SAVAGE FUTURE

SAVAGE FUTURE

The Sinister Side of the New Age

Kenneth R. Wade

Autumn House®
HAGERSTOWN, MD 21740

Copyright © 1991 by Autumn House® Publishing Company

The author assumes full responsibility for the accuracy of all facts and quotations as cited in this book.

This book was
Designed by Bill Kirstein
Cover art by Helcio Deslandes
Typeset: 11 pt. Palatino

PRINTED IN U.S.A.

96 95 94 93 92 91   10 9 8 7 6 5 4 3 2 1

AH Cataloging Service
Wade, Kenneth R.
    Savage future: The sinister side of
the New Age.

    1. New Age Movement. 2. Religion—
New Age. I. Title.
                150.19

ISBN 1-878951-10-6

Dedication

I dedicate this book to my wife, Debby, and my sons Adam and Seth, without whose patience and prayerful support I couldn't have stayed in my study (the dungeon) for enough hours to complete it!

Contents

CHAPTER
1

How I Met the Feathered Serpent

A chill ran down my spine as I climbed the hill that the conquistadors, foreign conquerors of the Aztecs, called Cerro de las Estrellas—Hill of the Stars. I knew that this place had once been considered holy—a sacred killing ground, to be more precise.

It was August 7, 1989, and just moments earlier Pastor Joel Salazar-Otañez had parked his brown Volkswagen beetle at the end of Avenida Cinco de Mayo on the south side of Mexico City, the megalopolis that has grown up around the site of the ancient capital, Tenochtitlan. A large sign in Spanish indicated that the hill beyond the road's end was an ecological preservation zone. But I saw nothing to indicate the full significance of the zone or what lay at its heart.

I breathed in deep lungsful of the thin air, nearly 8,000 feet above sea level, and hefted my heavy camera bag onto my shoulder so I could capture on film the remains of an ancient pyramid whose significance for the New Age movement is unparalleled.

The date was significant for two reasons. First of all, because of its relationship to my own research into the

New Age movement. It was shy by just one week of being 11 months from the day I had completed the manuscript for *Secrets of the New Age,* a book Penny Wheeler and Richard Coffen of the Review and Herald Publishing Association had asked me to write. It quickly became one of that publisher's bestsellers for 1989.

After I finished the manuscript, I fulfilled several longstanding requests for magazine articles about the movement and then tried to put New Age things out of my mind. I felt I had been too deeply immersed in exploring the movement for too long. So I broke off contact with the New Age leaders whom I had befriended and tried to return to a normal pace of life. I even deshelved about 30 of the more than 100 New Age-related books that had crowded my library and stored them away in a box.

But several events that came together in the middle of 1989 undermined my decision and drove me to the conclusion that I must write a sequel to *Secrets of the New Age.* I had stumbled onto startling information that drastically changed my understanding of the New Age movement and where it could lead the world. In a flash of insight I came to realize that certain important aspects of the movement have implications more ominous than anything I had come upon before—implications that most people within the movement do not recognize and that few Christians understand. Yet these influences are changing our world even now, and their impact may grow until it rips apart the very fabric of our lives. These sinister influences first came to my attention when I discovered what had happened atop Cerro de las Estrellas more than four centuries ago.

At that point I had only begun to uncover evidences of the frightening future that New Age influences could lead to. In the coming months the true implications of New Age philosophy in relation to the Aztecs would become clearer to me. But for now I could only speculate.

And I certainly didn't want to get carried away in my speculation. I have often strongly criticized those Christian authors who have become alarmist in their writings about the New Age movement. I could not accept their speculative declarations that pointed to every New Age wishful thinker as a covert Nazi out to take over the world and destroy Christianity. I appealed repeatedly in voice and in print for Christians to maintain a restrained stance toward the New Age movement without being receptive to its ideas.

Yet the events of this summer had compelled me to begin asking some hard questions about where the paradigm shift that New Age leaders talk about is taking us. I began to wonder whether the New Age fascination with ancient religions such as the Aztecs' could lead to practices as repugnant as that which had happened here on Cerro de las Estrellas. My questions were based not only on this fascination with things from the past, though. Something much more basic to this highly touted paradigm shift deepened my concern.

The New Age movement calls for a paradigm shift—a change in our basic assumptions about life. With its emphasis on reincarnation, evolution, monism, pantheism, and progression of spirits, this shift is (perhaps unwittingly) changing the perceived value of each individual's life. The New Age worldview calls for society to consider your life and mine as merely one expression of the life of a spirit that needs to live and die in countless bodies in order to achieve enlightenment.

Actually the paradigm shift calls for us to begin to view human spirits as if they were aluminum soft drink containers—something that can and should be recycled!

Later research would reveal to me the awful consequences that such a view of life has had historically. But for now I could only wonder about what had happened on this mountain and what it might mean for the future.

Looking for Answers

The questions that came to a head during the summer of 1989 form the basis of this book. If you have read *Secrets of the New Age*, you will find this book quite different. (It is certainly not necessary to read *Secrets* first. But in a few instances in this book you will find references to background information given there.) The difference in style is because *Secrets* was a factual explication of what the New Age movement is. As such, it needed to be heavily documented with quotations and citations to demonstrate that I was not just expressing an unfounded opinion. In this book I go beyond a description of what the movement is and present my reactions to what I believe the movement is doing to our world.

If tomorrow you crossed a highway and suddenly noticed a Peterbilt truck barreling toward you at high speed, it would take just a fraction of a second for the basic description of the perpetrator of the crisis to embed itself on your mind. But the descriptive details would be relevant to you only insofar as you came to recognize that the Peterbilt's approach affected you personally and required you to take action.

Similarly, this book is about implications. It is not so concerned with relaying factual details as it is with my assessment of the details, especially as I have examined the New Age paradigm shift in the light of Bible prophecy. I have, for instance, often wondered how the events predicted in Revelation 13 (institution of religious laws that demand death for the disobedient) could ever take place in our secularized society. After you have read this book, you will know why this question no longer perplexes me.

What you read may at times seem frightening. I have

not written these things to cause unnecessary alarm, but when the implications of what I saw "coming down the pike" became clear, I could not keep silent.

Where It All Began

My renewed concern about the New Age movement's implications started with a letter from my good friend Mark Finley. Mark is an American evangelist who was working in Europe at the time. In May 1989 he wrote to me from England to tell me that he had encountered a lot of New Age influence in Europe. He asked whether I would be interested in putting together a slide program that could help pastors and evangelists acquaint people with the New Age movement.

I knew I was too busy to undertake such a project. I really had no relish for doing further New Age research. And besides, I wondered, what sort of pictures could one take of the New Age movement?

I had attended several New Age events and had photographs of crystals, people (including big-name celebrities) doing the dance of T'ai Chi, and a lady wearing a power pyramid on her head while she manufactured crystal jewelry. I had even tried to take a picture of a modern witch wearing her black cone hat, but she refused to be photographed. Could I put these and other photos like them together in a program that would be informative as well as interesting?

Then one day in July another evangelist, Carlos Aeschlimann, a South American who has spent much of his life working in Central America, stopped by my office. He knew that I was planning to attend some meetings in Central America and wanted to suggest things that I should see along the way.

His list included one of the world's finest anthropological museums, located in Mexico City, and the ruins of ancient Indian civilizations in Mexico and Guatemala. I thanked Carlos for his suggestions, although I doubted that I would have much time to play tourist on this trip. Then a staff meeting agenda came across my desk and reminded me that in a couple days I would be presenting Mark Finley's letter to our staff and asking whether or not I should pursue his suggestion that I prepare a slide presentation.

Suddenly I realized that my two evangelist friends' ideas meshed like gears in a Swiss watch. Carlos wanted me to visit Mayan and Aztec ruins and a museum that contains displays dealing with humanity's ancient forms of worship, while Mark wanted me to supply slides related to the New Age movement.

Carlos' recommendations had answered my questions about Mark's proposal, because much of some people's hopes for the New Age is founded on looking back to ancient religions such as those practiced by the Indians who inhabited North, Central, and South America prior to the Spanish conquest. In fact, the most widely publicized New Age event ever held—the Harmonic Convergence of August 16, 1987—was a direct product of study of the old Mayan Long Count calendar.

So I went to staff meeting armed with the evangelists' ideas. Our staff quickly approved any minor stretching that my travel budget might require to enable me to get the photographs for the New Age program.

Eight days later I sat in a hotel room in Mexico City as I pored over background material about pre-Columbian civilizations in the Western Hemisphere—a subject I knew almost nothing about.

It was there that I became acquainted with Quetzal-coatl, the feathered serpent god who dominated the ancient Americans' lives. Pieces of information I had gathered in years of research for other projects fell into place to form a collage, and I felt impelled to write this book. I wanted others to see what I had come to perceive—those deeper, serpentine roots of the New Age movement that threaten, perhaps promise, to turn it from what some consider a benign fad, or even a beneficial paradigm shift, into a potent force that demeans the value of human life.

CHAPTER

2

The Mountain and the Murders

Thunder boomed in the distance as Joel and I trekked toward the top of Cerro de las Estrellas. "The Indians used to run to the top of their pyramids," Joel informed me.

That's fine for them, I thought, *but they weren't lugging 20 pounds of camera equipment. And undoubtedly they were a good deal better acclimated to the thin air of the altiplano than I am.*

We were both aware we were climbing a hill that had been climbed by thousands of other people intent on something very different from our mission. In fact, at least once every 52 years the climbers had included the highest priests of the kingdom, who accompanied a man chosen to be the sacrificial victim. The Aztecs believed the victim's death would ensure the continuation of life for the universe.

Throughout the land on this most sacred of their days, the Aztec people waited anxiously to learn the results of the New Fire ceremony on the Hill of the Stars. They waited in town squares, in temple precincts, but not at home. They had broken all their furniture, cooking utensils, and idols and had extinguished their cooking fires.

16

For five days they had lived in mortal fear that the universe would collapse about their heads, extinguishing life. Their only hope lay in the successful completion of the rituals taking place on the Hill of the Stars.

Their dual calendar formed the basis of all this. One calendar, called the astronomical calendar, divided the year into 18 months of 20 days each, with five unlucky days at the end of the year. Their second calendar, which they used for astrological and divination purposes, had only 260 days in its year. These two calendars synchronized once every 52 astronomical years. That is, New Year's Day was the same day in both calendars once every 52 years. So the Aztecs, like the Mayas who originally formulated the calendars, believed that they entered a new era at the end of every fifty-second year.

If at midnight on New Year's Eve the priest succeeded in kindling a fire up there on the mountain, then the sun would rise on the morrow and the universe would continue its normal rhythms for another 52 years.

But in Aztec belief the sun needed something more than a bonfire to give it strength to awaken the next morning. They believed that the sun's very lifeblood was *human* blood. For the New Fire to be efficacious, it needed to be accompanied by a libation of blood. So the pyramid atop Cerro de las Estrellas did not have just an ordinary hearth for the fire. It had an altar on which a man could be stretched out and bound down so he could be the receptacle for the kindling and the fire. The Aztecs believed that if the victim went to his death willingly and stoically, he would be privileged to serve the sun god in heaven and follow his chariot across the sky for the rest of eternity.

The Aztecs celebrated the New Fire ceremony for the last time in 1507. [1] Later, in 1521, Spanish conquistadors led by Hernan Cortes overthrew the Aztec Empire and placed statues of the virgin Mary in their shrines.

Cortes destroyed most of the structures in the sacred precinct of Tenochtitlan, the Aztecs' capital city, and took stones from their pyramids to build a Christian cathedral nearby. The pyramid atop Cerro de las Estrellas fell into disuse, and for centuries no one paid any attention to the Long Count calendar. No one bothered to offer sacrifices at the top of the pyramid. But in the 1980s an art professor by the name of Jose Arguelles resurrected the Long Count calendar and, through calculations too abstruse for anyone but the most dedicated chronologists to understand or critique, arrived at the conclusion that the next Mayan Long Count would end with the winter solstice in the year 2012. And that this would not be just any old Long Count, but the end of the Great Cycle that the Mayans taught had begun at the creation of the universe.

What's more, Arguelles taught that on the night of August 16, 1987, the world would transition from the series of nine 52-year hell cycles that began on the very day that Cortes landed in Mexico into a series of heaven cycles. [2]

Around the world, people who were hoping for something better for our world in the third millennium A.D., or in the Age of Aquarius (into which astrologers believe we are moving right now), pricked up their ears and began to listen to Arguelles. Maybe he had something there, some New Age leaders opined.

How many bought in to Arguelles' chronology is impossible to know, but on August 16 and 17, 1987, tens or perhaps hundreds of thousands (Arguelles believes it may have been millions) of New Age believers converged on what they called spiritual power points around the world. They gathered together, held hands, meditated, and chanted or hummed the Hindu primal word *Aum* in hopes of bringing peace to earth in what Arguelles believes is the last half of the last Long Count in the Great Cycle.

This was the Harmonic Convergence—the most touted New Age event in history. Ironically, its call for peace and harmony centered on the date for one of the most gruesome ceremonies practiced by one of the most brutal and warlike peoples ever to populate our planet. And devotees who gathered together on this day reported seeing signs and symbols of Quetzalcoatl (the great feathered serpent) in the sky! [3] And no wonder—those who follow Arguelles' teachings believe that beings from outer space founded the Mayan race and started the Great Cycle calendar, and that these same beings will return in the 1990s to prepare the world for the New Age, to dawn in 2012 at the beginning of the next Great Cycle. [4]

For those who understand the New Age movement, the irony of expecting peace based on the Mayan calendar comes as no surprise. As with every fad that has caught the popular imagination in recent years, most of the practitioners know next to nothing about the basis of what they do. They simply go along with the crowd, doing what others are doing, basing their practices on sketchy information, rumors, and faith in their leaders.

But the New Age movement is no flash-in-the-pan fad. It did not end on August 17. Rather, it continued to expand in popularity, attracting more and more attention. Today many observers of our culture concur with New Age author Marilyn Ferguson, who calls the New Age transformation a paradigm shift and "the most rapid cultural realignment in history." [5]

Concern with where this realignment is taking us led me to Cerro de las Estrellas just about two years after the celebration of Harmonic Convergence.

At the top of the mountain I had hoped to find a tall pyramid like several others I had examined and climbed during the preceding two days. I had expected to find signs and a display detailing what the Aztecs had done here and why. At the very least I had expected to find some stone serpents—ancient gods—like the one I had found at every other pre-Columbian center of worship I had visited in Mexico.

I was disappointed to find only a half-dozen steps, perhaps 40 feet wide, constructed of rough stone and mortar. The rest of the pyramid had been carried away to provide foundation stones for more recent building projects. Seated on the steps was a group of Mexicans who had climbed the hill for a family outing. They laughed and chattered happily, seemingly oblivious to the sinister origin of the works on which they sat. They seemed puzzled and a bit amused that a gringo would pack so much camera equipment up here and take so many pictures of this tumbled-down monument.

The storm that had been a mere rumbling now boomed and flashed directly over Mexico City. The combination of smog and haze was so thick that we could not see the skyscrapers only a few miles away.

"This would be a bad place to be in a thunderstorm," I said to Joel in broken Spanish. He quickly agreed, for Cerro de las Estrellas is the highest point for miles around.

For my purposes, however, the crashing thunder and flashing lightning proved helpful, because the picnickers on the pyramid shared my opinion about the merits of getting caught in the storm there. They vacated the steps, allowing me to photograph the remnants of the pyramid standing silent and barren against the darkening sky.

The New Fire ceremony was only one of the multitude of human sacrifices carried out regularly by the Aztecs, Mayas, Incas, and other Native American tribes. But these people were not alone in their passion for offering human blood to their gods. My research in coming weeks would reveal that human sacrifice has been practiced in almost every culture at one time or another.

Sacrifice Here?

Below me the world's largest city sprawled on every side. And I wondered whether human sacrifice would ever again be practiced on the Hill of the Stars. I wondered, too, whether human sacrifice might be going on at that very moment somewhere among the 20 million residents of Mexico's Federal District, who, on a clear day, could see this mountaintop.

My questions were not unfounded, as a brief look at one of the most gripping Mexican news stories of 1989 makes clear. The story began in Miami in the middle sixties, but its roots go back much farther, to religions that originated in Africa and in the New World and have been melded with Roman Catholicism to yield the religions called Santeria and Palo Mayombe. It is estimated that as many as 100 million people in the world practice Santeria.

Growing up in Florida in the late sixties, Adolfo de Jesus Constanzo (born in Cuba) learned the basic principles of Santeria. These principles festered and grew in his deranged mind until they erupted in a wicked boil that cost the lives of 17 or more young men, including himself and his best friend.

In those early days in Miami, Adolfo learned to deal with his enemies by leaving decapitated chickens or geese on their front porches. From Miami he moved to Mexico City. His reputed powers as a *curandero,* or healing witch, ingratiated him to even the wealthy and influential of the city, opening the way for the establishment of a prosperous drug-running enterprise. In 1987 or 1988 he visited Haiti, and that may be where he added the practices of the Palo Mayombe religion to the repertoire of his increasingly violent behavior.

All these influences came together in Adolfo's apparently psychotic mind to yield horrific results that no one would have believed possible if what happened hadn't been so carefully documented in photographs and the testimony of Adolfo's associates.

The results were discovered by Mexican police in April 1989 in a rundown shack 20 miles west of Matamoros, Mexico. Votive candles, railroad spikes, a bloody machete, and a horseshoe on a chain lay scattered about on the blood-smeared floor of a room whose central feature was an iron kettle filled with spikes, a roasted turtle, and a charred human brain.

Shallow graves here and at a nearby farm yielded the remains of 15 young male sacrificial victims, including Mark Kilroy, an American college student who had been kidnapped in Matamoros on March 14. The trail of evidence and testimony led from there across the border to Brownsville, Texas, where Adolfo's witch friend Sara Maria Villareal Aldrete was an honor student at Texas Southmost College. And from there back across the border to Sara's home, where police found a makeshift altar near a blood-spattered wall. And finally to Mexico City, where Adolfo and Sara were holed up in an apartment with six members of their drug-running gang. There Adolfo became the final victim of his deadly blend of religion and crime after ordering a gang member to shoot him and his closest friend.

As the story behind the deaths unfolded, police learned that Adolfo and Sara had been the leaders of a gang that believed they could be protected from the police, and even from death, by sacrificing the lives of other people. Whether more victims died as a result of their belief may never be known, but the discovery of baby clothes in Adolfo's home makes it seem likely that his first human victims may have been infants who were sacrificed right there—within sight of Cerro de las Estrellas.

The Meaning of What Happened at Matamoros

One of the most significant aspects of this story is that the perpetrators of these heinous crimes—the people who kidnapped and sacrificed other human beings in the name of their religion—were not superstitious peasants or a group of Indians practicing ancient rituals. They were thoroughly modern, well-educated, likable, powerful people who had simply allowed the powers of darkness to take over and rule their lives. Through a combination of greed, drug running, and lust for power, they became caught up in a horrid satanically inspired practice that sane, rational, educated people such as you and I tell ourselves we could never permit, let alone perpetrate. But my later research would reveal that it is intelligent, inquisitive young people who most often are attracted to the type of satanic worship that calls for human sacrifice.

I also learned that human sacrifice is more the norm than the exception in human history. The idea that gods can be fed or appeased, or that special powers can be attained, through the ritual killing of another human being runs like a scarlet thread throughout the warp and woof of human history. This, along with the idea that death is merely a doorway to another life—no doubt the reasoning that led Adolfo Constanzo to have himself and his best friend killed—has led to countless premature deaths in our world. The concepts that lead to human sacrifice seem to hold a far-too-prominent place in the human psyche.

Why is this? And is there a chance that this instinct, repressed now under the veneer of civilization, could become a part of normal life once again?

Chapters 4 through 8 will present evidence from a number of movements that, along with the New Age movement, are growing in power today and are leading to the devaluation of human life. These movements have brought questions about the possible renewal of human sacrificial ceremonies to the forefront in my mind. But before we examine the current scene, we need to understand why human sacrifice has been so widely practiced in our world.

CHAPTER

3

Human Sacrifice: Doing What Comes Naturally

When the king of Ur died in 2550 B.C., 63 people— soldiers, musicians, nobles, servants, and concubines—carried small golden cups down a steep ramp into the pit that had been prepared for his final resting place. When the procession ended, each of them quaffed the poisonous contents of the cup and sat down to die.

As their eyes closed in death, other servants began the long process of filling the burial pit with earth. Those charged with sealing the tomb deposited a layer of clay over the crypt and tamped it smooth to form a floor. On this floor the priests who had officiated at the funeral sacrificed animals and another man—perhaps in the belief that his spirit would guard the tomb from grave robbers.

Before the ghastly job of laying the king to rest was finished, several more layers of earth had been poured in, and several more "floors" had been consecrated by the deaths of human victims.

In China the practice of burying attendants with their master survived into the Sung Dynasty (A.D. 960-1279).

When Inca Roca, sixth king of the South American Inca Dynasty, died 500 years ago, many of his wives and concubines hung themselves by their own hair.

As Adolf Hitler prepared to shoot himself on the afternoon of April 30, 1945, Eva Braun, his faithful companion and wife-for-a-day, demonstrated that the ideas prevalent in Ur had not disappeared from the human psyche. Although what she did could not be considered human sacrifice of the same genre practiced in Ur, it seems to me that the similarity of these practices, separated by nearly 3,500 years, is significant. Braun, like the ancient women of Ur, swallowed poison in order to join her husband in death. Two days earlier Benito Mussolini's mistress Claretta Petacci, had also chosen to stick with her man to the end and died at his side.

When American religious leader Jim Jones determined that his community should commit suicide in 1978, nearly a thousand of his followers played follow the leader and drank juice laced with cyanide.

When Adolfo Constanzo knew that he was about to be captured by police in 1989, he ordered Alvaro de Leon Valdez to shoot both him and his best friend, Martin Quintana Rodriquez. The two men entered a small closet together to await the hail of bullets that would end their lives—and presumably, in Constanzo's belief, send them to a future life together.

Someone once said that the more things change, the more they stay the same. Because even as mankind seems to advance by developing new technologies, new ways of looking at life, and new strategies for survival, the one thing that doesn't change is human nature. Though we may think of ourselves as urbane, civilized, and intellectually advanced beyond the level of the savages who once practiced human sacrifice, the stories of Braun, Petacci, the Jonestown victims, and Constanzo's friend call into question such a claim.

HUMAN SACRIFICE

Ritual Death Around the World

The examples just cited illustrate that one type of human sacrifice has been an acceptable option for some throughout recorded history. But this is only one type of human sacrifice. Other types carried out for various reasons on victims willing or unwilling have been important parts of culture from the Arctic to the equator, and on every inhabited continent of our world.

In India, for example, the Hindu religion has traditionally called for human sacrifice. The case of the Khonds of Orissa, in Bengal, eastern India, is one of the best documented and most illustrative cases of regular ritual human sacrifice that was carried on well into the nineteenth century and then was stopped only by forceful British intervention.

The Khonds went so far as to keep a sort of brood of people, called Meriahs, in their villages to be sacrificed each spring at the planting season. They treated the Meriahs well throughout their lives, gave them land to raise crops on, and allowed them to marry and raise families. But each year, when it came time to plant their crops, they selected one or more of the Meriahs to serve as the sacrificial victim whose body would be used to assure success of the crops. They took the Meriah to a sacred grove and killed him in as slow and painful a manner as the human mind could conceive.

James Frazer described the process in his famous work *The Golden Bough*. His description is based on eyewitness accounts. "In one district the victim was put to death slowly by fire. A low stage was formed, sloping on either side like a roof; upon it they laid the victim, his limbs wound round with cords to confine his struggles. Fires were then lighted and hot brands applied, to make him roll up and down the slopes of the stage as long as possible; for the more tears he shed the more abundant would be the supply of rain. Next day the body was cut to pieces."[6] Pieces of the body would then be buried in fields as a sacrifice to the mother goddess and to assure good crops. (In chapter 7 I will deal with the return of mother goddess worship in New Age circles. Keep this bit of information in mind for application at that time.) In other areas the Meriah would first have his limbs broken, and then he was carted about from house to house throughout the village to give each head of a household the opportunity to cut off a piece of flesh for his field.

The motivation for this sacrifice repeats a theme echoed round the world and heard wherever people depended on agriculture for their sustenance. As Joseph Campbell, one of the world's leading authorities on mythology and religion, put it, "out of the rocks [out] of fallen wood and leaves, fresh sprouts arise, from which the lesson appears to have been that from death springs life, and out of death new birth. And the grim conclusion drawn was that the way to increase life is to increase death. Accordingly, the entire equatorial belt of this globe has been characterized by a frenzy of sacrifice—vegetable, animal, and human sacrifice."[7]

It was against such sacrifices to assure fertility and prosperity that the biblical prophets railed. The Phoenicians, with whom Kings David and Solomon had treaties and business dealings, and from whom King Ahab took his infamous wife Jezebel, were notorious for their child sacrifices. Excavations at Carthage, the Phoenicians' most famous colony, have uncovered hundreds of urns filled with charred babies' bones. Archaeologists estimate that 20,000 or more children were burned alive as sacrifices to the goddess Tanit and her consort Baal during one 200-year period. And sacrifices occurred there regularly for nearly 600 years.[8]

The Aztecs of Mexico frequently sacrificed 20,000 or more victims to their sun god in a single year. And here, too, suffering formed an important part of the ritual. Often the priests extracted the victim's still-beating heart from his chest and held it up as a votive gift to the sun.

The Mayas too, from whose calendar the New Age devotees who celebrated the Harmonic Convergence get the dates for their celebrations and expectations, delighted in extracting beating hearts. They adorned the walls of their temples throughout Central America with paintings depicting victims being held spread eagle on a convex stone while a priest performed "heart surgery." (I don't mean to imply that everyone interested in Mayan religion wants to reinstate human sacrifice. Fascination with ancient religions is just one influence among many within the New Age movement that leads toward devaluation of human life.)

European observers, such as the famed British explorer Sir Richard Burton, reported that during an average year in the West African kingdom of Dahomey 500 human victims would be sacrificed to the memory of deceased rulers, but that during the year a king died the number could rise as high as 1,000.

However, human sacrifice was by no means the prerogative only of savages living in the deep, dark jungles. It was a part of life in Greece (where it was not condoned, though probably practiced from time to time), Rome (where it was infrequent because it was viewed as unacceptable), China, Japan, Scandinavia, and among the North American Indians.

The Romans may not have sacrificed as many children as their archrivals, the Carthaginians, but they certainly were not beyond offering a human sacrifice. The great emperor Augustus once sacrificed 300 men on an altar dedicated to his predecessor Julius Caesar. And the superstitious Nero sacrificed a number of noblemen when he felt his own life threatened by the appearance of a comet. As late as the third century A.D. the historian Porphyry reported that a man was sacrificed every year in Rome at the feast of Jupiter Latiaris. [9]

Unlike Rome and Greece, all over Europe human sacrifice was more the norm than the exception. The Celts, who conquered much of the continent during the first millennium B.C., would place war prisoners and criminals inside huge wicker images and set them afire. The historian Tacitus wrote that "they deemed it indeed as a duty to cover their altars with the blood of captives, and to consult the gods through human entrails." [10] Unfortunately, even a cursory examination of New Age literature reveals a great New Age fascination with Celtic religion.

While in a few societies it may have been considered an honor to be sacrificed (some would maintain that the ritualistic offering of human sacrifices reflected the high value placed on human life, because a human sacrifice represented the very best, most valuable, and most potent offering possible), the fact is that most societies sacrificed the most powerless individuals within the culture—slaves, prisoners, women, and children.

The Germanic peoples believed that their god Odin needed to have new subjects sent his way via regular sacrifices. Typically, his subjects were selected from among enemy warriors. [11] So important was this aspect of warfare that Nigel Davies, author of many books on Central American religions and one on human sacrifice, has postulated that "possibly the very origins of tribal warfare lies not in the need to punish or pillage but in the demand for captives to sacrifice." [12]

A lesser-known but widely practiced form of sacrifice persisted well into the Christian Era in Europe and into modern times in Burma. This was the practice of burying a live victim in the foundation of a new building in order to propitiate the deity whose land was being disturbed and in the hope that the person's spirit would watch over the building. For similar reasons both the Vikings and the Polynesians placed human beings on the rollers used to launch new ships. The human blood reddening the keel was an offering to the sea gods.

In India the rama of Mewar continued the practice of sacrificing a man to the god of the river Mahi until 1828. The man would be killed and his corpse thrown into the current before the rama crossed the river—apparently with the intent that if the river god was hungry for human flesh, it could be satiated with a sacrifice instead of claiming the rama's life.

Why So Much Sacrifice?

The rituals of human sacrifice, and the reasons given for the sacrifice, vary from culture to culture. But few cultures can claim that none of their ancestors killed people for religious reasons.

As I have read of dozens of human sacrificial rites, I think that I have detected one underlying factor or motive in all of them. No matter what the stated reason for sacrifice, the basis I sense behind it all is a kind of "me or thee" reasoning—a kind of substitutionary sacrifice.

In all my reading I have uncovered no evidence that any group sacrificed human victims capriciously—just for the thrill of watching them die. Even the Aztecs, who have the reputation of being perhaps the most brutal and extravagant sacrificers of all times, had what seemed to them a valid rationale for their activities. They believed that the sun required human blood to sustain it in its daily journey across the sky. Furthermore, they believed that a person who died willingly as a sacrifice to the sun would be privileged to follow that god in his course across the heavens for all eternity.

In essence, then, the Aztecs sacrificed to the sun god in order to preserve their own lives, for they believed that if they failed to offer up enough victims, the sun would wane and no longer grace them with light and heat. On one level it meant feeding the god and thereby renewing his power and keeping him happy. On another level I think it was a simple "me or thee" bargain. Either the sacrificial victims died, or the whole nation would ultimately die.

In other instances a tribe would sacrifice one or more victims in the hope of averting plague, famine, or pestilence by propitiating the gods for the sins of the community. On other occasions and in other cultures human sacrifice was carried out on criminals and was a penal sacrifice by which the community was purged of wrongdoing.

Other human sacrifices were seen as gifts of gratitude for past benefits or for future benefits anticipated from the deity. In ancient Carthage, for example, many of the infants burned for the goddess Tanit were given to her in fulfillment of a vow the sacrificer made regarding what he or she would do if she gave a certain blessing.

Yet it seems to me that the same selfish motivation runs through every form of human sacrifice known to historians, although sometimes the stakes were lower on the "me" side than the "thee" side. For instance one of the oldest Vedas (the sacred writings that form the basis of the Hindu religion) prescribes the number of human beings that must be sacrificed to fulfill such mundane things as the lust for wealth or the desire for supremacy over others. The latter required the sacrifice of 11 people. [13]

Of course, the cases of those who were killed in order that they might follow their masters into the next realm involved the lowest stakes on the "me" side, for the person demanding the sacrifice was already dead yet could still exercise enough control to require others to die in order to somehow continue to bless the "me" even in death.

Thus millions of human lives have been sacrificed by people with the power to decide the fate of others in order to preserve or simply enhance their own lives. It seems that the fate of the individual has been regarded as of less significance than the fate of the collective whole. As I see it, the root cause, then, of human sacrifice is human selfishness. And if there is one characteristic of humanity that has not been subdued through the years, it is selfishness.

Human Sacrifice Today

The Adolfo Constanzos of the world, who believe that special powers may be achieved by killing others, are fortunately a minuscule minority in our world today. But is that because the motive force that drove people to sacrifice others has abated? Or is it simply held in check by a thin veneer of civility—or by the common person's revulsion to the sight of blood?

Is it possible that Revelation 13, with its depiction of a religious power that will call fire down from heaven and require the deaths of all who will not accept the mark of the beast, may actually point to a time just before the end when human sacrifice will be reinstituted?

These questions have no simple answer, but clues abound in the record of nations' and individuals' treatment of one another.

The record of Germany under the Nazis is one of the most obvious clues. Some see it as simply the story of a nation that succumbed to the madness of its ruler. But the real story, despite its many tales of heroism and self-sacrifice on behalf of the persecuted, is a chronicle of millions of human beings who, faced with the choice of standing up for the rights of others at the risk of their own lives, chose to remain silent. There was no ritual here, no cherished hope that the gods would smile on them for letting others be hauled away to their deaths. Instead, we find simply an attitude that if there's a choice of who must die, it is "better thee than me."

But the atrocities of Nazi Germany are only one example of what lies at the heart of humanity in crisis. More recent examples from Cambodia, Colombia, Uganda, Lebanon, Ireland, the Soviet Union, and even downtown America flash daily before our eyes, screaming their message that when push comes to shove, the average human being's reaction is that death is better for thee than for me!

So the killing goes on. This is not human sacrifice per se. The stated motivation has changed. But in reality the basic "me or thee" motivation still raises its ugly head.

Nigel Davies, at the conclusion of his 290-page book about human sacrifice from earliest history through the Jonestown massacre, becomes philosophical. He ponders whether the urge to kill other humans is not so deeply ingrained in our psyche that it is necessary to fulfill it either through ritual or, in the absence of that, through war or crime. Pondering this, he makes a startling suggestion: "Faced with the mass brutality of our century, real as well as simulated, one may ask whether, in its place, man might not do better to revert to the ritualized killings of the past. If the need for scapegoats persists, could this not be met with less bloodshed through the medium of a solemn ceremony, in which one stoic victim meets his end on the god's altar, dying with dignity for the common good? If violence is endemic, sacrificial violence is at least a more restrained form." [14]

A startling suggestion indeed! But fortunately only one scholar's isolated musings.

But there are forces operating in our world today that help make such ideas palatable to more and more people. We will look at some of these in the next chapter. And because the quotation I cited above is not the end of his comment on the matter, we'll be back for one more visit with Dr. Davies. The rest of what he has to say will become relevant after we consider the information in chapter 4.

CHAPTER

4

What Is a
Life Worth?

Without a drastic shift in thought patterns in the Western world, human sacrifice could never again become part of mainstream culture. Nigel Davies points this out in the conclusion to his book *Human Sacrifice in History and Today*. Today we are obsessed with the prolongation of the individual's life, no matter what the cost.

Thus, in the United States it is necessary for families to fight long court battles if they want a hospital to disconnect life-support machinery from a brain-dead loved one. Street-dwelling derelicts who want to succeed at suicide must take their drug overdoses in isolated back alleys to avoid being rescued, resuscitated, and returned to the existence they had chosen to abandon.

But a reaction against such heroic measures has already begun. In some European nations euthanasia (mercy killing of the terminally ill or of those who are simply tired of living) is becoming acceptable, although it has not yet, to my knowledge, been legalized. And in America a physician has created a death van with an apparatus designed to aid the terminally ill in killing themselves painlessly.

For the most part, though, the religion of the day is anthropocentric. That is to say, Western society places the value of the individual human life at the center, and it musters all society's resources for preserving that life.

The basis of this anthropocentrism is secular humanism. But disillusionment with humanism is growing as people become aware of its spiritual barrenness. It leaves a person groping after something spiritual to fill the vacuum in his or her soul. As I pointed out in *Secrets of the New Age*, this groping has opened the way for what New Age writers call a paradigm shift that is changing the way people view the world.

In the course of research for that first book about the New Age movement, I felt that I achieved quite a comprehensive grasp of the roots of the movement and where it was headed. But what I learned in Central America helped me realize that the impact of this paradigm shift goes deeper than I had thought. It affects the way even those who have never heard of the movement live. And if its influence goes unchecked, it may affect the way millions die!

Monistic Pluralism

The human mind never ceases to amaze me. In many ways it is like the mixing bowl my wife uses in the kitchen. I've watched her throw together what seems to me simply an odd assortment of ingredients into the bowl and stir it up. But when she is finished, the odd assortment always comes out looking and tasting in accordance with a magnificent master plan.

The brain is like that—always picking up odds and ends of information. Many of these tidbits are seemingly forgotten, but somewhere along the line something happens that triggers a thought, and then the odds and ends start coming together in a pattern, and you end up with an insight that makes it look as if all the pieces were part of the recipe in the first place.

In order for you to understand the product of my cogitations about the New Age movement, you need to know about a couple more ingredients that went into the stew in my mind.

Two important things happened to me on February 12, 1989. But they didn't seem particularly significant until nearly six months later.

That Sunday I presented my press credentials and was welcomed warmly by the staff of the Heart to Heart Festival, in a government auditorium on Constitution Avenue in Washington, D.C. I knew that such New Age notables as Marilyn Ferguson, Barbara Marx Hubbard, Sir George Trevelyan, and Sri Chinmoy had come to speak to this gathering, so I quickly made my way to the press/celebrity lounge to see whom I could meet. Fortunately I was able to arrange interviews with several New Age leaders, but it was a serendipity that proved most meaningful in the long run.

While in the lounge I struck up a conversation with Mr. David Polland, who was in charge of publicity for the event. Also in the lounge at the time was actor Dennis Weaver, who had come, he told me, chiefly as a favor to the sponsor. I hadn't really planned to interview Weaver, since I didn't think of him as being particularly closely involved with the New Age movement. But Mr. Polland assumed I might be interested in an interview, so when he introduced me to Weaver, I quickly formulated a series of questions.

We talked about the New Age movement in general and his view of it, and then I began asking questions about his view of the world. As we talked, I noticed a man sitting halfway across the room, listening avidly. When I asked Weaver whether he thought people were basically good or evil at the core, the man across the room broke into our conversation with an obviously deeply held conviction. "There is no such thing as good and evil," he said. From then on, we had a three-sided conversation, but the ideas of the man across the room dominated the rest of the interview. He and Weaver agreed about the nature of our world—that the world is a unity and we can choose to live selfishly or unselfishly, but that in the end nothing is inherently good or evil.

Douglas Groothuis, one of the most erudite and fair-minded outside observers of the New Age movement, has written that "the idea that 'all is one' is foundational for the New Age; it permeates the movement in all its various manifestations—from holistic health to the new physics, from politics to transpersonal psychology, from Eastern religions to the occult. Another name for this idea is *monism*." [15] Part of the belief system that comes with monism, Groothuis points out, is belief that "good and evil are really one and the same." [16]

This same idea found expression in a most intriguing way an hour or so later at the Heart to Heart Festival. About a thousand people had gathered in the main auditorium to hear Al Huang's presentation, titled "Harmonizing Your Whole Self—A Dance of T'ai Chi."

Al Huang was introduced as an emissary of joy and harmony who travels and presents his programs both in the United States and in China. It soon became evident that Mr. Huang's presentation would not be any dry lecture about harmony. Clearly a kinesthetic person, he soon had the whole auditorium involved in the dance of T'ai Chi—raising their arms heavenward to draw power from above, then reaching downward to form roots and draw stability from below.

I felt conspicuous for my lack of participation, but then I've been known to sit quietly through the histrionics of a charismatic church service as well. And I sensed a strong similarity between what Mr. Huang was doing and the technique used by some evangelists to get a crowd fired up.

Al was perfectly charming. His Chinese accent and idioms added a spice of humor and a bit of irony to everything he said. And he soon had everyone leaning when he leaned, stretching when he stretched, bending when he bent, breathing when he breathed, and holding their breath when he held his. You couldn't help liking him and wanting to join him in his one-man mission to break down the barriers between the Communist and capitalist worlds.

He kept up a cheerful banter all through the exercises. And just about midway through, he began to talk about the Chinese year. He wanted us to know that the year of the dragon had just ended and the year of the serpent had just begun. By now he had the crowd eating out of his hand, drinking in every thought he shared with them as they mirrored his every movement.

And it was then that the most extraordinary thing happened. All through the dance the only sounds that had come from the crowd were occasional titters of laughter and the sounds of bodies moving in unison, feet stomping on cue, and such.

But now, having hit upon the topic of the serpent, Huang diverged into theology. "Serpent is the feminine quality of the masculine dragon," he said. Then he gave his explanation of the role of the serpent in Eden. "There may be wisdom behind that serpent asking Adam and Eve to bite the apple. The serpent may be God's partner— teaching us something. When Adam and Eve started making excuses, God and serpent are winking at each other—OK?" The sense of innocence portrayed by his Charlie Chan accent belied the weightiness of his ideas.

But the amazing thing was not what Al Huang said. It was the crowd's reaction. All over the auditorium spontaneous applause broke out when he asserted that God and the serpent were partners.

They had applauded him when he came onto the stage. And they applauded him when he left. But this was the only comment he made that evoked spontaneous applause.

Snake Worship

I found the crowd's reaction curious, even fascinating. But it was just one among many ingredients stirring around in my mind, awaiting the clue that would bring them all together in a way that made sense. What I learned about Quetzalcoatl and the Aztecs and human sacrifice and the Mayan Long Count proved to be that clue.

I grew up in a Christian home, and was taught from an early age that there is a God in heaven but that He has an archrival called the devil, who took over the body of a serpent and tempted Eve to eat the fruit that gave her knowledge of both good and evil—obedience and rebellion—and caused her and Adam to be driven from their garden home. The eventual result of succumbing to the words of the serpent and rebelling against God was all the sin, sorrow, and troubles that we see in the world today.

Inherent in the Bible's account of the fall of Adam and Eve is the implication that because the serpent served as the instrument of temptation, God took away its original powers and cursed it to crawl in the dust of the earth. Through the years Bible interpreters have seen in this curse the implication that the serpent was not originally limited to crawling in the dust but may have had the ability to fly.

Mythologies around the world are filled with accounts

of winged serpents called dragons, and even evolutionists see a close relationship between reptiles and birds. My college ornithology textbook described feathers as specialized scales!

The Bible implies that once the serpent became identified with the devil and his evil schemes, God stripped its feathers and left it to crawl in the dust.

So I grew up believing in a real God and a real devil, who was God's archrival, not His partner. But when I was about 10 years old, a man I knew became convinced that there is no such thing as a devil and that the real cause of sin is simply that we tempt ourselves.

I was too young to understand that there was any real danger in such a teaching, but those older and wiser than I assured me that one of Satan's favorite strategies is to persuade people that he does not exist so that they will lower their guard against him. But no amount of arguing, reasoning, or persuasion could change the mind of my friend. Worse yet, he became an evangelist for his new ideas, talking to and trying to persuade everyone he knew.

Finally one day, having exhausted all human resources to get through to the man and show him that his new ideas were erroneous, a group of us had a season of prayer, asking God to take away the deception that was clouding this well-meaning person's mind. Although the man never knew about the prayer season, his change of mind was instantaneous. His ideas about the nonexistence of the devil evaporated, and he never mentioned them again. So I grew up believing in a real devil, who is a devoted enemy of God and who is symbolized by a serpent that once had feathers.

When, in my hotel room in Mexico City, I learned about the Aztecs and other American Indian tribes' worship of feathered serpents, I began to have suspicions about the origins of feathered serpent worship. I wondered whether it might harken back to a vaguely remembered story of Eden. The fact that Quetzalcoatl, the feathered serpent god, was known as the god of knowledge seemed to tie it to the serpent's role at the tree of knowledge. And the fact that he was also associated with Venus, an ancient symbol of Lucifer, gave an added clue.

I began to wonder if the choice to worship the serpent had come about through a decision by the tribes' ancestors to cast their lot on the side of the serpent and Satan rather than on the side of God. And might that decision by any chance have any relationship to the brutal forms of human sacrifice that formed the basis of their religion?

Subsequent study revealed a startling correlation between serpent worship and human sacrifice. Serpent worship and human sacrifice have gone hand in hand throughout history. And the correlation certainly stands to reason. Satan's chief motivation is the destruction of human life. And he's an expert at leading those who worship him to carry out his plans.

Moreover, human sacrifice is a natural outgrowth of the rejection of God and the substitutionary sacrifice He has provided in His Son. I'll have more to say about that in chapter 9.

The Two Shall Be One

Another enlightening detail became evident in the following days as I visited Aztec and pre-Aztec pyramids and toured the Mexican National Museum of Anthropology in Chapultepec Park. The predominance of the serpent symbol at every pre-Columbian sacred site strengthened my conviction that this symbol's importance harked back to some ancient memory of Eden. But the added significant detail came when I learned that the Aztecs' Templo Mayor pyramid, the centerpiece of Tenochtitlan, their capital city, actually had two temples and altars at its summit. The two temples represented the uniting of the dualities, the blending together of good and evil. They stood for the concept of monism that is becoming so popular again under the New Age movement's influence.

The serpent worshipers of Tenochtitlan, then, were proclaiming the exact same message as Al Huang and the man who interrupted my conversation with Dennis Weaver and all the New Age devotees who spontaneously applauded the idea that the serpent and God are really cooperating.

But Al Huang was not drawing his ideas from the Aztecs. His ideas about the essential unity of all the powers in the universe come from his Oriental background. And no one who understands the New Age movement will deny that Oriental religion has had a profound effect on New Age devotees' understanding of life. Their monistic outlook comes from Eastern religion. Belief in reincarnation also comes from Oriental religion, and, as I pointed out in *Secrets of the New Age*, is one of the most widely held tenets of New Age believers.

Now it's time to bring Nigel Davies, the expert on human sacrifice, back into the discussion, as I promised I would at the end of chapter 3. Near the beginning of *Human Sacrifice in History and Today*, Davies scrutinizes several theories about why human sacrifice has been such a common practice in so many cultures. One theory holds that killing humans is just a stage that all civilizations go through on their way to becoming more enlightened. But Davies takes issue with this theory and uses the example of what happened in Rome as a prime example of its fallacies. "In Rome," he writes, "human offerings almost ceased and then increased in number again in the wake of Oriental cults that became popular under the empire." [17]

Whoa! If that didn't make you sit up straight, blink, and shake your head a few times, you need to go back and read that last sentence again. The Oriental cult in Rome was Mithraism, which comes from the same Vedic roots as Hinduism.

Few people know what a baleful influence the influx of Oriental religion has had in the past. And as George Santayana said, "those who do not remember the past are condemned to relive it."

The New Age leaders who have traveled to India to sit at the feet of swamis and gurus in recent years have not encountered the reality of Hinduism. What they have seen is a watered-down version whose true character was suppressed by the British overlords' enforcement of laws against human sacrifice. And Davies points out that sacrifice was banned in India once before in history—when the Buddhist religion subjugated Hindu practices. "But once Buddhism had been expelled from its homeland, sacrifice was promptly revived." [18] The implication here is that human sacrifice is an integral part of Hinduism that may be suppressed but probably cannot be eradicated from its foundational belief system.

An interesting side note that I came upon while reading a New Age-oriented magazine is that while suttee—the burning of a Hindu wife after the death of her husband—is now outlawed in India, the practice of wife burning is still prevalent there. Only now it is young newlywed wives who are being purposely burned to death by husbands who have collected the dowry and have no further use for their wives. [19]

But wait, there's more.

It would take more than the influx of a little Oriental philosophy to shake our society free of its fixation on the preservation of life. To quote Davies again: "At the root of human sacrifice lay a belief in a hereafter that was not unlike life on earth. . . .

"Only in the world of today has death been demythologized. It has become a separate state, divorced from life, and we strive obsessively to save the dying from crossing this great divide. Once people share the belief that this life is the be-all and end-all of their existence, ritual sacrifice must abate, regardless of what other forms of killing take its place." [20]

New Age philosophy removes this obstacle from the path back to sacrifice as well by promoting belief in reincarnation.

These evidences alone would not be enough to convince me that we need to worry about the reemergence of human sacrifice. Chapter 5 unveils other forces that seem to be opening doors that lead in that direction.

CHAPTER

5

Are We All One?

The way people think about life—the basic ideas that motivate their decisions—is changing right before our eyes. The paradigm shift that the New Age speaks of is real.

We see it in the newspaper headlines: "Man Kills Ex-wife, Then Shoots Himself"; "Ex-employee Kills 13 at Printing Plant"; "Best Friends Die Together in Suicide Pact." Such news stories were far less common in the days when most people believed in an all-seeing, all-knowing God and in a future existence in either heaven or hell. Belief in reincarnation, with its chance to work out one's problems in a future life, has made murder and suicide a much more palatable option for some. For others, belief that death is the end of all existence has opened the doors of their minds to think of suicide as the best way out of a seemingly hopeless situation. And the idea that there is no such thing as good or evil has helped free people from any moral constraints that might have deterred them from violence.

Hell Versus the New Age

It may have been only a coincidence, but I saw a pattern in it. At a New Age convention I attended in early 1989, I struck up conversations with a number of participants. Several told me that they had turned from Christianity to New Age belief because they could not accept the idea that God passes judgment on people and rewards or punishes them according to their deeds. Somehow these people found the Eastern concept of karma, which teaches that we can atone for misdeeds in the present life in a yet-future life, more acceptable.

Karma is basic to all Eastern religious thought. It can be expressed simplistically in the proverb "What goes around comes around." In other words, it teaches that in the end all things must be balanced out.

The Eastern concept of origins teaches that in the beginning everything in the world was a part of Brahman—the creator god. Individual entities came into being when certain spiritual entities split off from Brahman. As they split off, they became aware of their individuality and began to behave in selfish ways because they had become unconscious of their oneness with all creation. In their separateness, then, they began to concentrate more and more on physical existence and forgot that they had a spirit that was really one with the universe—just one small part of Brahman.

According to this view, the real goal of life is not to concentrate on the physical, but to become aware of your spiritual side and your unity with everything and everyone else. By concentrating on this spiritual side, you will advance beyond self-centeredness and begin to perceive your oneness with the universe. The ultimate goal of life is to perceive this fully and then to be reabsorbed into Brahman and cease to exist on the physical plane. To achieve this, one must live multiple lives and learn important lessons from each life—try it again and again until it's gotten right. After you've learned all the lessons and gotten it all right, the law of karma will no longer compel you to come back and live again and again.

Ironically, according to New Age thought, the way to achieve this non-self-centeredness is through inward-focused meditation.

While the previous paragraphs oversimplify the working of karma, it is the version that New Age writers popularize today, with this exception: New Age teachers typically modify the goal of multiple lives to include greater and greater enlightenment and existence on higher and higher planes instead of mere absorption into Brahman.

The goal of life, according to this teaching, is to realize that you are just a part of all the world around you and that it is a part of you. At first glance it seems that such a teaching would help bring about peace on earth and goodwill toward humankind. It implies that if I will just learn to recognize that the person I think of as an enemy is really an extension of myself, the sense of enmity should melt away like the edges of butter pats in the summer sun. And that if I but come to recognize that the trees of the forest and the chipmunks and the squirrels are as much a part of divinity as I, then my desire to exploit the earth's natural resources will evaporate.

But the outworking of this belief system is not as beneficent as you might expect.

New Age writers who promote this worldview like to cite the example of the American Indians, who lived in harmony with their environment rather than exploiting it. Because the Indians thought of the bison as sparks of the divine—just like humans—they treated the bison with respect and killed only as many as they needed. And when they killed a bison, they had an elaborate ritual that they believed atoned for their actions and invoked the great bison spirit to continue to bring the herds to supply the needs of the Indians.

Those who admire this model fail to perceive that you can't bring the bison up to par with humans without taking humans down to the level of the bison. Therefore, in the end this belief system makes the death of a human being no more significant than the death of a bison.

The animal rights movement also draws on monistic belief. And here it certainly seems to have a benign, if not beneficent, effect. It teaches that because the guinea pig or monkey is really one with me, I should not treat it in inhumane ways. Much of the current protest against using animals in medical experiments is founded in this belief that animals are sparks of the divine and deserve the same sort of respect we give to humans. While I'm all for treating animals humanely, the philosophy that makes the life or death of my son no more important than that of a dog is repugnant and dangerous.

This belief in the oneness of all creation also plays a part in the ecology movement. One prominent New Age leader told me that while such organizations as the Green Party, which is active in ecology in Europe, are not a direct part of the New Age movement, they are doing what New Age believers should do. The Green Party promotes ecology for secular reasons—to preserve our planet for future generations. But the New Age movement imbues the same ecologically oriented actions with spiritual significance. The New Age influence filters into the secular side of the ecology movement through the concept of Gaia.

Gaia (or Ge) is the name the Greeks gave their Earth goddess. Hence the prefix Geo in such words as geology and geography. *Gaia: A New Look at Life on Earth*, a book published by the Oxford University Press in 1987, took a scientific approach to the idea of earth as a sentient being capable of responding to ecological crises by adjusting her temperature or atmosphere to compensate and preserve life. An earlier book entitled *Gaia: An Atlas of Planet Management* (New York: Doubleday, 1984) details the ecological crisis our world faces.

It seems inevitable, though, in this age of spiritual seeking, that these scientific works would be appropriated and given a metaphysical significance. So the scientific community's interest in the earth's ability to preserve itself has been translated, in New Age minds, to justify a return to belief in the great mother goddess of primitive religions. I'll have more to say about this and its application to feminism and even witchcraft in chapters 6 and 7.

Having said what I have about ecology and animal rights, I must hasten to add that just because a cause or movement gets linked to the New Age movement does not mean that the cause is bad, or even that it is really part of the New Age movement. Many non-New Age causes get caught in the movement's broad shadow without partaking of its form.

The Dark Side of Oneness

Rudimentary to New Age belief in the oneness of all is the belief taught in the *Star Wars* movie trilogy. In these movies George Lucas introduced us to Luke Skywalker and Darth Vader—two men who have chosen to operate on opposite sides of something called the force. This force, we come to understand in the course of the story, is the unified field of energy that empowers the whole universe. But it has both a dark and a light side, and those who choose the dark side become involved in murder, piracy, and all sorts of evil. On the other hand, those who choose to operate on the side of light are kind, considerate, and helpful to others (but they still end up killing a lot of people and wreaking a lot of destruction as they battle those on the dark side).

The proper aim of life in this arcane scenario based on Eastern religious philosophy is to achieve a state of oneness with the light side of the force and thus to become an immortal in the manner of Obi Wan Kanobi, who died in the first movie yet continually returns in spirit to instruct young Skywalker. (It is never made clear why a person could not just as well become one with the dark side and thus become immortal while frowning instead of smiling.)

The happy ending to the trilogy comes when even Darth Vader surrenders to the power of love and oneness, as represented in his son Luke, and rejoins the struggle on the side of light—and right.

New Age channels [21] have picked up on this light/dark motif and use it to authenticate their ministry. In *Opening to Channel*, channels Sanaya Roman and Duane Packer counsel those who would like to become channels by making contact with beings from other dimensions to be careful not to be led astray by unenlightened beings who might want to make contact. They provide a simple test to be applied to all beings who might try to channel their wisdom through the person who is opening to channel: simply ask the being whether he or she is "from the light." The authors assure their readers that the beings will not lie, and they counsel that if the spirit being admits that he is not from the light, the channeler should tell the being to go to the light. After breaking contact with the being who is not "from the light," the channeler may continue his or her searching until contact is made with a being who claims to be from the light.

Roman and Packer's counsel hardly seems sagacious, because Satan himself is known as "a liar and the father of it" (John 8:44, NKJV) and Lucifer (which means "light bearer"). So those who try to connect themselves with what they think of as a source of light and truth may actually begin receiving their information and instructions from the prince of darkness, aka the father of lies.

Where Monism Leads

So there is danger in accepting the belief that the universe is controlled by a single force and ignoring the presence of good and evil supernatural forces.

But the depth of the danger doesn't become apparent until you start making the logical applications of this philosophy of oneness. Along with belief in its philosophical concomitant reincarnation, monism has the potential to drastically alter the way we think about and treat human life.

The Hindu belief in monism, karma, and reincarnation—with all its promise of beneficence—has not led to peace, harmony, and love. And this paradox began to dawn on me as I had opportunity to visit parts of the world where Hinduism is widely practiced.

In Singapore I stopped to contemplate the artwork at a Hindu temple. I was rather taken aback by the depictions I saw there of some of Hinduism's deities. I, like many American baby boomers, had grown up with an image of Hinduism as the ultimate of pacifist religions. *Why, then*, I wondered, *do Hindu artists picture its gods in fierce-looking poses?* Later on the island of Java I photographed some Hindu murals in a meeting hall. Here also the Hindu heroes looked fierce and swung mean-looking scimitars at one another.

How could a religion whose gods looked so cruel be the kind, peace-producing religion I had come to think that Hinduism was?

Actually my perception, not the reality of Hinduism, was askew. For, as we saw in chapter 4, Hinduism's history is anything but benign. Hinduism historically encouraged human sacrifice. It was the Christian British who suppressed human sacrifice in Hindu India. And in ancient Rome the infiltration of ideas from Oriental cults similar to Hinduism brought about an upsurge in human sacrifice after it had almost died out.

How can this be? How can a philosophy that teaches the unity of all lead humans to abuse, neglect, torture, and kill one another?

The answer becomes clear once you understand the true implications of monism, karma, and belief in reincarnation.

Here's one way to look at it: karma teaches that whatever happens to me in this life is a result of something I did in a previous life. It also teaches that if I suffer in this life, this suffering is preparing me for a more beatific life in the future. Therefore, if I see someone suffering, it is no concern of mine. If I were to relieve the suffering of an outcast on the street, I would be interfering with his karma, and he would simply have to live another life of suffering to make up for the pain he missed in this life.

Add monism and reincarnation to belief in karma, and you get a worldview that sees each life as just a small, insignificant, temporary spark of the overall oneness that is god. When viewing human life from this perspective, one might feel justified in concluding that people are no more important or valuable than gnats.

Taken to a logical conclusion—though by no means the only possible logical conclusion—such a worldview justifies wars, murder, and human sacrifice. If you consider all creation to be part of one body, then it is the right of the larger part of the body to decide the fate of smaller parts.

Consider what happens to your body when you trip and fall. Automatically the individual body members begin to work together to protect the body as a whole. The hands rush forward to take the brunt of the force of your fall and to protect your head. Perhaps a shoulder comes up to take the force as you roll over on your side. Each part of the body instinctively sacrifices itself for the preservation of the whole.

By the same token, if one part of the body becomes cancerous or gangrenous, it is the prerogative of the rest of the body to decide to have the diseased part excised in order to preserve the life of the rest of the body. And this is precisely the basis on which human sacrifice has been carried out throughout the centuries. The idea is that the suffering and death of one part of the body is necessary on a regular basis in order to preserve the life of the rest of the body.

This, coupled with belief in reincarnation, can be construed to justify the torture inflicted upon a sacrificial victim prior to his or her death. The experience of suffering and death that the victim undergoes is simply a doorway to a new existence. And, having suffered so gravely in this life, the victim can expect a better life in the future. So for someone who espouses this perspective, the torturers are really doing the victim a favor!

This, then, is the dark side of the oneness doctrine. If we are all but a part of one great whole, it doesn't matter what happens to the individual. What is most important is the prosperity of the body as a whole. In an environment conditioned by such a belief system, no one individual's life is safe.

And it is not only in religious systems that such principles can become active. Naziism and Communism in Germany, Russia, China, Cambodia, and other countries have led to the preeminence of the rights of the state over the rights of the individual. In the Soviet Union under Stalin this resulted in the deaths of as many as 50 million citizens by starvation, death marches, and banishment to labor camps. Was the motivation really so different from what drives people to human sacrifice? I think not. In my opinion the "me or thee" mentality motivated each of these forms of killing.

Recently a Christian couple returned from a visit to Albania, at that time one of the most restrictive Communist countries in the world, and quoted a government official's explanation of why Christians were still being persecuted in his country. "The dissenter must be destroyed, like a weasel in the chicken coop," he said. [22]

But lest I leave the impression that only foreign governments and systems have fallen into this trap, I must hasten to admit that good old American capitalism has had similar effects whenever capitalists have allowed profits to take precedence over human life.

Human sacrifice has taken many forms throughout history. In a secular society its form is different from that found in a religious society. But the results—at least for the victim—are the same.

What can prevent us from falling into this trap once again? Does Christianity have anything to offer to keep us safe? In the next chapter we will contrast the New Age view of the value of humanity with the real value that God has placed on human lives.

CHAPTER
6

Real Value
for Real People

In *Return to the Garden*, Shakti Gawain, one of today's most popular New Age writers, tells a compelling story of the origin of life on earth. It is a takeoff on the biblical story of Adam and Eve in Eden. The variations Gawain works on the Genesis account shed a lot of light on how New Age thinkers apply the monism/reincarnation/karma/spiritual evolution theme.

In Gawain's story all things began as one, but then at some point the oneness began to separate into male and female, which released energy. Sometime later a wise old snake (Quetzalcoatl, the Mayan/Aztec god of knowledge, perhaps) taught the female to eat a special fruit and then to get the male to do the same. This action resulted in enlightenment, released energy, and began the process of further separation. But soon the separate beings began to forget their essential spiritual oneness and focused too much on the material world. The challenge, according to Gawain, for those who wish to return to the garden and to overcome their separateness and be reunited, is to become enlightened about their spiritual unity and to be redeemed from concentration on the fragmented material world.

Salvation, according to this account, results from enlightenment. Belief in salvation by enlightenment is foundational to much of New Age thought. But it is certainly not a new belief system. Salvation by enlightenment lies at the root of Buddhism, Hinduism, Gnosticism, and many other ancient religions.

But Christianity offers something much better. In fact, biblical scholars recognize that much of the New Testament directly attacks Gnosticism, a school of thought popular throughout the Roman Empire, which taught that enlightenment was the key to salvation.

What Really Happened in the Garden

The Genesis account of what happened in the Garden of Eden reveals a very different sort of God in action and a very different reason behind the creation of Adam and Eve.

According to the Bible, Adam and Eve did not come into being through some accidental spinoff of energy from a central power source. They were the culmination of a carefully organized and exquisitely executed creation plan. Their creation as separate, autonomous entities endowed with the power to make decisions about their own future was part of a divine scheme to increase the joy and love in the universe.

The tempter in the tree was not cooperating with God in a plan to enlighten Adam and Eve. The serpent was given the ability to speak by the rebel angel Satan, not by God. To borrow New Age terminology, the serpent served as a channel—but not for some beneficent being on a higher plane. It received its words directly from the center of rebellion against God's gracious plan for His creation.

God allowed the rebellious tempter a place in Eden, not to enlighten Adam and Eve, but as part of His plan to strengthen their will and their ability to make wise choices.

When Adam and Eve chose to rebel against God and eat the forbidden fruit, they and their descendants did indeed begin to lose track of the spiritual elements in their lives. But the spiritual element referred to by the Bible is something different from the New Age concept of spirituality.

Shakti Gawain and other New Age leaders teach that the way to rediscover the spiritual is through an inward journey: "Each person has to wake up and connect with the inner nature and learn how to live in harmony with it," Gawain says. [23] On the other hand, the biblical account makes it clear that Adam and Eve's spiritual experience in the garden focused outward, not inward. When they wanted to contact God, they did not assume a lotus position, chant a mantra, and wait for some ethereal presence to manifest itself within their minds. Why would they want to do that when they could walk and talk on a physical level with the very real God who had created them?

They did not seek mystical union with some abstruse, unctuous entity that could manifest itself only to their inner eye. They reveled in the fascinating experience of discovering the individuality God Himself had granted them and encouraged them to grow in.

Even after they lost their innocence and had to leave the garden, they and their descendants continued communicating with a real God outside themselves. The temptation to look inside themselves for God was of the same nature as when the serpent said "Ye shall be as gods" (Genesis 3:5). Throughout Scripture God is portrayed as being external to humanity. For instance, Enoch and Noah "walked with God" (Genesis 5:22; 6:9). Abraham came to know God and even held face-to-face communication with Him (Genesis 18).

"Enlovement"

Through the years, as people became acquainted with God, they discovered that what God wanted for them was not so much enlightenment, but "enlovement." "God so loved the world, that he gave his only begotten Son, that whosoever believeth in him should not perish, but have everlasting life" (John 3:16). That is the rallying cry of those who proclaim this good news. The gospel focuses on individuals and what God has done to redeem them from destruction and give them the privilege of maintaining their individuality throughout eternity.

God's goal is not that His created beings be reabsorbed into Himself. That would make His original plan in Creation nothing more than a costly foible with net results of zero. No, He created Adam and Eve—and you and me—in order that we could learn to love Him in response to His love. And in learning to love Him, we learn to love others as well.

This love for others is not based on the New Age concept that once I become enlightened I will discover that everyone around me is just an extension of myself and that I naturally must love them because they are part of me. The gospel teaches that each individual on our planet is a unique, autonomous creation of God, that God loves all His created beings despite their recalcitrant sinfulness, and that God's goal is to redeem each one to live eternally in a sinless world.

In coming to know God and becoming like Him, it is my privilege to discover the unique individuality of those around me and, by the infilling of God's grace, to learn to love them with all their quirks and eccentricities. My quest is not to unite them with myself, but to love them even though they are different from and totally separate from me—to help them even though doing good for them may not bring any direct benefit to me.

The route to this enlovement is not through focusing inward to discover the better me inside. No, no! The gospel is painfully honest. It reveals that what abides in my inmost nature is *not* loving or unselfish. Far from it. By nature I am self-centered and can love only myself. Jesus pointed out that the thoughts and motivation that abide in our hearts are neither enlightened nor loving by nature. "What comes out of a man, that defiles a man. For from within, out of the heart of men, proceed evil thoughts, adulteries, fornications, murders, thefts, covetousness, wickedness, deceit, licentiousness, an evil eye, blasphemy, pride, foolishness. All these evil things come from within and defile a man" (Mark 7:20-23, NKJV).

The apostle Paul also points out that by nature we are in rebellion against God and good, and that only the action of the Holy Spirit on our lives can bring us into harmony with God's good plan for our world. (See Romans 7:18-8:11; cf. Galatians 5:16-26; Ephesians 2:1-10; 4:17-29.)

But God is not content to leave me self-centered and rebellious. As His Holy Spirit comes to me, He works changes in me, teaching me to love my neighbor as myself, mollifying my meanness, and making me like my Creator in the ability to love the unlovely. He teaches me to see others, not as potential enemies, but as living vessels into which He Himself wants to be poured, and from whom He wants to shine forth giving love to others (see Matthew 5:43-48; 1 John 4:7-21).

When I see those around me as potential reflectors of the image of God—no matter how marred, mauled, and miscreant they may be—I can love them. Whereas New Age philosophy might lead me to believe that the handicapped, the violent, and the ugly are merely defective parts that need to be excised from the oneness and given the privilege of incarnating in a better being later; the gospel teaches me to view each one as a candidate for developing God's love and for living eternally in that love.

An Encounter With God

The story of Abraham's encounter with God helps me understand what God wants for each of His created beings.

Abraham was born and raised in Ur about 500 years after the great tomb for the king and his 65 retainers mentioned in chapter 3 had been sealed. Archaeological evidence indicates that the practice of worshiping the king as god and sending his servants on to the "next world" with him via sacrifice was still being practiced when Abraham walked Ur's streets.

But Abraham heard and answered the call of a different sort of God—One who was interested in him as an individual, not just as an extension of some earthly lord whose purpose on earth would end at the death of his master. God called Abraham to find his identity in God and in God's promises for the future.

Abraham's response was at first little more than tentative. In fact, a careful reading of the account in Genesis 11-25 reveals that Abraham's father, Terah, first responded to God's call and that Abraham apparently just went about his own business until he himself experienced a call from God—at age 75! (In the first part of the story Abraham is called Abram. God changed his name to Abraham later, when He promised to give him a multitude of descendants.) God called Abraham to leave his home and to journey to a land that God would show him because God wanted Abraham to learn to rely on divinity instead of on himself to provide for his future.

We typically think of Abraham as a man of exemplary faith who set out trusting wholly in God. But truth be known, the Bible story does not concern a saintly old gent who never wavered or questioned. By studying the life of

Abraham in the light of recent archaeological discoveries, we learn that when he left Haran to journey to Canaan he stopped by Damascus on his way. And not just for a visit. While there he apparently made arrangements to borrow some venture capital to help him establish his family business in the new territory. This explains why Eliezer of Damascus was his sole heir later in life (see Genesis 15:2). The Damascus bankers had a policy that anyone who borrowed money from them and went to another land must first adopt one of their men as his heir in order to ensure repayment from the borrower's estate in the event of death.

The very basis on which Abraham accepted God's challenge to move from his home and go to an unknown country was God's promise to bless him with offspring and to bless all the world through his descendants. The only problem was that he had been married for many years, but without children. It seemed clear that either he was unable to father children or his wife was barren.

Knowing this, his journey to Canaan becomes almost a last-ditch effort to achieve, by answering God's call, what he had been unable to do on his own. Yet when Abraham arrived in Canaan, he did not suddenly become a father.

He stopped first near Shechem, and there he received God's promise that He would give the very land where he stood to his descendants. But for the time being the land was already populated by the Canaanites (Genesis 12:6). So Abraham moved on south and stopped at Bethel. Even though he built an altar there and called on the name of the Lord, he received no further message from God.

With his faith under trial and no direct evidence of God's actual blessing in response to his obedience, Abraham resorted to doing what seemed best to him, without seeking any further divine counsel. It seemed impossible to stay in Canaan because of a famine, so instead of remaining where God had promised to bless him, Abraham journeyed even farther south.

Finally he ended up in Egypt.

The story of his shady dealings in the land of the Nile is well known. First of all, he convinced his beautiful half-sister wife, Sarai, to pass herself off as just his sister. He didn't want to risk his life defending his wife from the pharaoh if he wanted to take Sarai for his own wife.

But after reading the story carefully, I wonder if there wasn't another reason in the back of Abraham's mind. Is it possible that this was just a polite way of giving Sarai her walking papers? Did he figure that he needed to get rid of Sarai if he was going to be able to have children? Was Abraham even now scheming to find a way to help God fulfill His promise to provide a son to carry on the family name? Abraham's later attempts to help God along lead me to think that this may have been what he had in mind. Later he even went so far as to agree to take Sarai's maidservant as a concubine to bear a child for him.

The Journey Up Moriah

Not until Sarai had passed normal childbearing age did she finally bear a son for Abraham. I believe God waited that long to give Abraham a son by Sarai (who by that time had been renamed Sarah) as part of His plan to teach Abraham to rely on Him instead of in his own strength.

The story of Abraham is a series of vignettes in which the pilgrim who came to be known as the friend of God learns the same lesson again and again: God is your provider. He is the one who will ensure your prosperity now and in the future. Your own strength and wisdom— the power that resides within you and can be accessed through looking inward—is inadequate to fulfill God's marvelous plan for you. You must learn to rely on God, not yourself.

Thus all of Abraham's life was a preparation for the events that are related in Genesis 22 as the last major story about his sojourn in Canaan. And the account teaches a lesson most relevant to New Age philosophy.

Because now, at least a dozen years, and probably more, after Sarah had finally given birth to the promised son, Isaac, God came to Abraham one night and told him to take Isaac up into the mountains and offer him as a burnt offering—a human sacrifice!

Shades of Matamoros! Shades of Cerro de las Estrellas! Carrying kindling wood for a burnt offering, the man and his son climbed the mountain together. And now came the greatest challenge of Abraham's long life. The test for which he had been studying for more than a century.

The crux of the matter came down to one question. On whom would he rely for his future? In his society the wealth and future of a man were all bound up in his sons. They would carry on their father's name. They would represent his accomplishments to posterity. They would assure that their father would not be forgotten. They would take the wealth that he had garnered and multiply it. They would multiply his descendants and spread out over the face of the earth to claim the land that God had promised. And so Abraham looked upon young Isaac as the embodiment of his hopes and plans for the future. And not only that, the boy was the embodiment of every answer to prayer the old man had ever experienced.

But now the same God who had promised and provided the son was asking Abraham to offer Isaac up as a sacrifice. To offer up a son as a burnt offering to a god was not uncommon in those days. In fact, most religions, and even kings, required the sacrifice of sons as a routine part of worship.

The man and the boy stood on top of the mountain, and Abraham had to make a choice. All through his life he had sought to use the resources within himself to provide for his needs. Time and again he had failed to trust God. But time and again God had patiently shown him that it was in trusting that his needs would be fulfilled.

Now Abraham had to decide again whether to look within and to trust in the fruit of his own body for his future, or to trust in the God who had revealed Himself as outside of Abraham, distinct from the man but very able and willing to provide for his needs.

If he obeyed the command and sacrificed his son, he would be right back at square one in his life—having to rely only on divine promises. If he refused to obey and instead took his son back down the mountain, he would still have the tangible evidence of God's blessing in the past. But to keep it he would have to abandon the path of faithful obedience. And then what could he really count on for blessings in the future? On whom could he rely to fulfill the promises God had given to him for his descendants?

It was a classic choice—to look within or without for blessing.

Abraham chose to trust the God whom he had come to know rather than to rely on his inner instincts and abilities.

So it was that at the very instant when he was ready to sacrifice his son, a voice called to him from heaven. "Abraham! Abraham!" the angel said, "Do not lay a hand on the boy. . . . Do not do anything to him. Now I know that you fear God, because you have not withheld from me your son, your only son" (Genesis 22:11, 12, NIV).

And as Abraham looked up, he saw a ram caught in a thicket—an acceptable sacrifice provided in place of his son.

The story concludes with God's reiteration of His promise to Abraham and his descendants. Now, because Abraham had chosen the path of faith in God instead of in himself, God promised on oath to bless his descendants and to multiply them until they could no longer even be numbered.

The story of Abraham and Isaac lies at the very foundation of Western religion's opposition to human sacrifice. It also stands as a wall against the Eastern concept of turning within and looking to purely human resources.

It teaches us to look to a God who is wholly other from ourselves yet wants to bless us.

It teaches us to rely on the grace of God. For He can be trusted to provide.

It teaches us that each of us is a valuable individual—not just some insignificant drop of water in a sea of being.

It also teaches God's willingness to provide a substitute so that we need not practice human sacrifice. The animals offered in the Hebrew form of worship represented God's ultimate sacrifice of His Son as a substitute for the death that sinners deserve to die.

And it teaches that the future is important—that God wants to provide for it, not just to absorb us into Brahman or a state of nothingness.

These values have often been corrupted in Western society. Even the Christian church has been guilty of taking individualism too far and has been caught with its hands in the coffers, lusting after wealth and worldly gain for its leaders.

But these lessons continue to nag at our consciences. They surface in the concern that we show for the homeless, in the social aid programs carried on by our governments, and in the charities to which we give billions of dollars every year. They drive rock musicians who may never take the name of God on their lips except in cursing to donate time and talent to concerts whose proceeds go to feed the starving in parts of the world where the people will never hear them sing, let alone buy their recordings.

Nonetheless, these values are under assault today. They are being undermined by the very paradigm shift that New Age leaders hail as a giant leap forward in human evolution!

But it is not just the New Age movement that is undermining these values. Many other influences that are growing in strength contribute to the decline of human values as well.

CHAPTER
7

Human Values
Down the Drain

As I sit in my office at home I can hear the television in the family room blaring the theme song for *Family Feud*. It seems hard to believe that by the time one of the contestant families has had their chance to win $10,000, nearly 1,000 other families will have lost a child to hunger or disease brought on by malnutrition. Or that since the program was on last night, 40,000 people have died of those causes. But the best estimates available say that this is the case. [24]

In some ways it seems as if our world is just too full of people. It seems impossible to care about all of them. Those of us who are living in prosperous areas are tempted simply to crawl into our shells, support strict immigration laws and a hefty defense budget, and ignore the plight of the 1.25 billion human beings who live in abject poverty.

But when we do so, are we not exercising the same sort of "me or thee" rationalization that we pointed out in chapter 3 as the basis of human sacrifice? Are we not simply saying "Let those people suffer and die out there; don't bring them here to spoil things for me"? By letting them die "out there" we preserve our universe, just as the

Aztecs did theirs. But our sacrifices have different priests. Their names are malnutrition and disease, and the cult that supports them is called neglect.

But wait, you say, can I really be held responsible for what happens in Ethiopia or the Sudan or Cambodia?

Perhaps not directly. But the very fact that we ask such questions is a symptom of something that has gone wrong in our world, something that has led to the devaluation of human life.

We see the starving faces, the displaced, the war-ravaged and wounded, on television and in the newspapers and news magazines every day. But in the magazines they garner our attention for only a moment, and then we turn the page to see the smiling face of a woman enraptured by Detroit's latest luxury offering, and we forget that the people we just read about lack even a place to keep dry during the monsoons.

After the television report of the latest disaster, a commercial comes on to remind us that we need to run out and buy a double whopper whimmy diddle while they're still on sale at K Mart. And at the end of the news program the anchor always relates a humorous or cheerful story to remind us that, really—at least for us—the world is not such a bad place after all. The tragedy and suffering we've just witnessed are not really serious. They were just pictures like those we've seen every day for the past decade. Life can go on as usual, and we need not do anything about what we've seen and heard.

For many people the violence they've witnessed on the news is not enough. They stay tuned for the evening network programs that bring knifings, strangulations, mutilations, and graphic portrayals of our inhumanity to each other right into the living room. Or if their cravings have moved beyond what can be shown on the broadcast channels, they slip a tape into the VCR or switch to a cable station that's playing the latest offerings from Hollywood's murder mills.

The Depersonalization of People

Do you know what an unperson is? That's what I call an extra who beams down to a planet with Spock and Captain Kirk on the popular television series *Star Trek*. A few years ago I went through a phase of relaxing with an episode of *Star Trek* every Saturday night for several months. It didn't take me long to catch on that some people were written into the plot of almost every program solely for the purpose of getting killed by whatever monster or alien life form was the enemy of the week.

They were always people the fans had never seen before and, of course, would never see again. They served merely as pawns in the game—someone to be sacrificed to allow room on the board for the big gun players to act their heroic parts.

Such is the fate of the extras in many a movie or television program. Viewers know it, expect it, and enjoy it. They go from one death scene to another, judging their relative merits on the basis of their realism and sanguinary detail.

It all seems like a normal part of society today, but only a few years ago most people never saw a violent accident in their entire life, let alone a macabre murder. Now children consider it commonplace to witness several fake homicides in the time it takes them to munch their way through a bag of Fritos.

Worse yet, now Nintendo, Sega, Atari, and other game manufacturers have made it possible for children to become not just viewers but participants in the video carnage. Take a look at the lessons taught by games ranging from the seemingly innocent Pac Man and Mario Brothers to the more blatantly violent ones, such as Rambo and Altered Beast. The message inculcated into millions of young impressionable players' minds is that the way to deal with opponents and obstacles in life is to knock them down, stomp on them, devour them, blow them up, or do whatever it takes to get them out of the way.

There is never time for negotiation or for treating the opponent as an individual whose rights ought to be respected and who could be reformed if treated with love and dignity. The message that bombards and becomes ingrained in video players' minds is that everyone who opposes me is unmitigatedly evil; I am always the good guy, and the right thing for good guys to do is to blow away the bad guys.

Will these young people, when they have grown up and taken over the reins of power in society, be able to divorce their actions in the real world from the strategies for coping that they practiced a million times on their television screens? I for one have my doubts. Will they be able to learn to treat enemy human beings with respect? Or will the primal urge to blow up whatever gets in the way reassert itself? Only time will tell.

According to my calculations, the first video game generation will be moving into seats of power around 2012—the year Jose Arguelles and his followers believe that the New Age will begin!

The point of all this is not to frighten people, but simply to point out that some of the most basic influences that affect the way we think are teaching us to treat others with less dignity than human beings created in the image of God deserve.

The Have-Not Gap

While this is going on, the gap between the have and have-not nations grows wider. And voices among the haves are calling for stricter immigration laws to make sure that the "huddled masses yearning to breathe free" don't pour in too fast and dilute the wealth we depend on to make us comfortable.

Add to this the problems engendered by the illicit drug trade, which, in many developing countries, portrays the message that the way to break out of poverty is through crime. And add on top of that the violence generated in the communities where drug running gangs carry on their turf wars at the expense of bystanders' lives.

In short, the influences that lead to the devaluation of human life are powerful, influential, and commonplace. But they have been held in check, at least in the Western world, by the basic value system of our society that has taught us that each person is an individual entitled to "life, liberty, and the pursuit of happiness."

While we may have learned to tune out much of the woe in the world, most of us still have a basic concern for the rights of others. But the New Age focus on oneness and reincarnation threatens to tear even these basic concerns from our hearts.

The best example of what Eastern philosophy, which forms the basis of New Age thought, does to human values can be seen on the streets of India, where Hinduism has been the reigning philosophy for thousands of years. In that land of castes and sacrifices, belief in karma, oneness, and reincarnation seems to be one of the factors that helps the upper classes to rationalize their disconcern for the plight of the outcastes. It appears as though some people have convinced themselves that if they were to interfere with karma by alleviating the suffering around them, the sufferers, who are paying their "dues" for wrongs done in a previous life, would only have to come back and suffer in another life to make up for the suffering missed in this life.

Such a belief system, when added to the already-rampant depersonalizing influences active in our society, can hardly be seen as a positive development for human values.

The Sinister Side

But the paradigm shift that is calling us to accept the Eastern way of looking at life is only one aspect of what the New Age movement is doing to change our value system. There's an even more sinister side. And it is this side that hit me as I sat in a hotel room in Mexico City.

Up until that time I had not drawn much correlation between the New Age movement and satanism. I had kept the two in separate camps in my mind. But suddenly the things that happened in Matamoros (see chapter 2) began to correlate with what had happened among the Aztecs hundreds of years earlier. And the Aztec fascination with serpents, such as Quetzalcoatl, the god of knowledge, began to correlate with what I knew about the very first New Age channel—the serpent who spoke for Satan in Eden.

I then began to realize that whereas the satanists may tune in to a more violent aspect of channeling and ancient religious practice and the New Age channels may be intentionally tuning in to aspects that instead speak of love and peace, in reality they are all listening to the same supernatural powers that are opposed to God's rule on earth.

When I first began researching the New Age movement, I was shocked at the openness of some in the movement to witchcraft, the occult, and ancient paganism. At the Library of Congress I came upon a book titled *Occult Preparations for a New Age* and a guidebook called *Pagan Occult New Age Directory*, designed to help people interested in New Age things network with groups that practice pagan religions.

As I pointed out in *Secrets of the New Age*, most people who identify with the New Age movement are heavily involved with crystals and other power symbols associated with pagan earth-related religions. But most of them would not confess to having anything to do with Satan or with his worship. In fact, many would deny that there is such a thing as a real, personal devil.

Even such para-New Age groups as Wicca (an organization of witches) are making a concerted effort to ensure that police officers understand that witches' supposedly benign rituals bear no relationship to the horrific accounts of animal and human sacrifice that have been attributed to satanists.

While there may indeed be considerable difference between most New Age neopagan rites and the satanists' blatantly murderous ceremonies, the fact of the matter is that the neopagans' apparent or real disassociation from satanism is irrelevant. Satan doesn't really care whether or not people acknowledge him by name. He simply wants to spark hatred, war, rivalry, or anything else that will serve his purpose of destroying people. He can work just as well through Nazism or the Irish Republican Army or Hezbollah or the Skinheads or the Medellin drug cartel as he can through satanistic cultists. As a matter of fact, he seems to prefer to carry out his most destructive acts through groups that do not claim his name or acknowledge his leadership. To inspire such acts openly under the name of satanism gives him bad press!

In other words, we may have less to fear at present from openly avowed satanists than from other groups that work according to Satan's plan without acknowledging it! To determine which groups these are, we need to understand some of Satan's background, plans, and motivation.

What Makes Satan Tick?

The Bible does not attempt to give a comprehensive description or analysis of Satan and his work. The passages that speak most clearly about him are Genesis 3 (although he is not mentioned by name here); the first chapter of Job; the Gospel accounts of his direct interaction with Jesus; allusions to his activities in Acts and the writings of Paul, Peter, and Jude; and the allegorical depiction of his activities throughout history as presented in Revelation 12. From these passages, along with Isaiah 14 and Ezekiel 28, we can piece together Satan's background and begin to understand what makes him want to bring about the devaluation of human life that makes murder and human sacrifice acceptable.

By piecing together the evidence from these passages, we learn that Satan began life in heaven and was known as Lucifer ("son of the morning," or "morning star"). In mythology he has been associated with the planet Venus, the brightest of the morning (and sometimes evening) stars. Perhaps the drama of the birth of each new day seems to recapitulate the struggle that went on between Lucifer and God. The ancients who lived in unlighted homes were much more aware of what went on in the sky than we are, and it is they who associated Lucifer with the star (actually planet) that often creeps over the eastern horizon a few hours before the sun, as if to announce that a new day will soon dawn. Day by day, year after year, those who hoped through the long nights for the sun to return, witnessed the climb of Venus into the sky. They saw it shine ever so brightly against the blackness of the night. It seemed to them many times brighter than any of the other stars as its radiance dominated the sky for those few short hours. But when the sun arose, Venus paled into obscurity.

In this daily drama people came to see a reminder of what had happened in heaven when Lucifer—the highest of the created angels—sought to ascend ever higher and even to stand in the place of God Himself. He rose up and did indeed outshine all the other angels. But compared to God, Lucifer's brightness paled into insignificance.

The prophet Isaiah pictured the Lucifer-versus-God drama in heaven in these words: "How you are fallen from heaven, O Lucifer, son of the morning! How you are cut down to the ground, you who weakened the nations! For you have said in your heart: 'I will ascend into heaven, I will exalt my throne above the stars of God; I will also sit on the mount of the congregation on the farthest sides of the north; I will ascend above the heights of the clouds, I will be like the Most High.' Yet you shall be brought down to Sheol, to the lowest depths of the Pit" (Isaiah 14:12-15, NKJV).

This poetic description, along with the other passages mentioned above, gives us a picture of a created angel who one day became jealous of God and, along with other disenchanted angels, formed a cabal intent on usurping the place of their Creator.

Revelation 12 tells us that as a result there was "war in heaven" and that eventually God cast Satan out of heaven. That is how he infiltrated the Garden of Eden, where he spoke through the serpent to tempt Eve. But the book of Job informs us that even though Satan had been driven from heaven as a result of his rebellion, he apparently had the privilege of visiting heaven from time to time. In fact, the story of Job 1 hints that beings from different parts of the universe assembled before God's throne in heaven from time to time, and that Satan represented Planet Earth because he had succeeded in tempting Adam and Eve to join him in his rebellion and thus had usurped Adam's claim as ruler and rightful representative of the earth.

But I've gotten ahead of the story a bit. After God drove Satan from heaven, this fallen angel went about seeking others to join his rebellion, and because Eve listened to his lies about God, life, and the forbidden fruit, this earth and the people on it became part of Satan's rebellion.

In what happened in Eden we begin to see the basic motivation underlying all of Satan's activity. There was no logical reason that he needed to tempt Eve, but rebellion had become a matter of principle with him. It wasn't so much that he needed more subjects as that he wanted to steal subjects away from God. It wasn't so much that he wanted to bring suffering to Adam and Eve as that he wanted to hurt God by injuring His creatures.

In fact, such is the animosity of Satan toward God that he will stop at nothing to hurt and malign Him. The real reason that Satan brought so much suffering upon Job and his family was to get Job to rebel against God. And as we can see from reading the story, although Satan didn't achieve his ultimate goal, he did succeed for a time in bringing reproach upon the name of God, for Job's various friends all attributed Job's sufferings to an act of God. Only because Job remained faithful to God and did not curse Him does a positive picture of God come out of this story.

Revelation 12 carries Satan's story a bit further by revealing that after Christ's resurrection and ascension Satan was once and for all thrown out of heaven and confined to this earth (see verses 7-12). By dying on the cross, Jesus caused the difference between God's love and Satan's hatred to stand out in such sharp contrast that Satan lost for all eternity his ability to deceive and rule the rest of the universe. Only on earth, where many people are unaware of the spiritual war between Christ and Satan, is Satan still able to carry on his deceptive, destructive work.

"Woe to the inhabitants of the earth and the sea! For the devil has come down to you, having great wrath, because he knows that he has a short time" (Revelation 12:12, NKJV) is Revelation's diagnosis and prognosis for our world in the years since Christ's victory over Satan. Satan directs his wrath against all who live on our planet because he knows that any pain or grief he can cause them will directly wound God's heart.

Satan's malignant machinations can best be carried out by people. So Satan works to teach people not to care about others. God, on the other hand, wants people to love their neighbors as themselves, to care not only about their own wants and needs, but about the needs of others (see Philippians 2:4-8).

Satan has a million ways to teach us not to care about each other. He tempts us to care more about things or work or hobbies. And he teaches us to think of our enemies as Japs or Commies or Krauts—or simply as one small, insignificant, temporary manifestation of one part of the great whole—instead of as individual human beings created by God to have hopes, dreams, loves, and passions like our own.

And if Satan can accomplish this goal so well through so-called normal influences, such as the modern media and longstanding nationalistic and religious rivalries, how much better can he accomplish it with people who purposely tune in to listen to his counsel?

In *The Devil's Web*, a carefully researched, nonsensationalistic book, Pat Pulling shares some of the information she has collected about satanically inspired murders in the seven years since her teenage son committed suicide as a result of contact with satanism. According to Pulling, even the Son of Sam murder case has been reopened, because newly uncovered evidence indicates that David Berkowitz did not act alone when he murdered 13 people in 1977, but was directed by a group of satanists. And convicted serial killer Henry Lee Lucas, who claimed to have killed 360 people between 1975 and 1983, admits that a satanic cult which made sacrifices to summon the devil ordered many of the murders. [25] On pages 45-50 of this same book, Pulling gives a sampling of 27 news stories gathered from newspapers all over the United States. They reveal a widespread pattern of crimes that include grave robbing, child abuse, sex orgies, animal sacrifice, murder, and human sacrifice—all committed, according to law officers (and sometimes according to the accused themselves), under the influence of satanism.

Satan and the New Age

When I wrote *Secrets of the New Age*, I did not see a direct correlation between the New Age movement and satanism. I kept the two separate in my mind because of the very different nature of their current activities. But if you've read that book, you know that in chapters 5 through 7, I make a strong case for believing that when New Age devotees begin channeling or seeking the advice of someone who does channeling, chances are good that they are receiving counsel directly from Satan and his rebellious angels.

The evidence is too strong to allow one to believe otherwise. Some channels are clearly tapping into some supernatural source. The sources, without exception, deny the existence of a devil, or at least deny that the devil is evil. They deny the reality of the war that started in heaven, and they relay precisely the same message the serpent gave to Eve in Eden.

So despite the apparent separation between New Age influences and avowed Satanist influences at present, the two are clearly tied in to the same source of information and inspiration.

Is it any wonder, then, that the unde
of the New Age—based on belief in rein
oneness of all creation—yields the same
tion of human life as does satanism? ... ...artetched
speculation to wonder whether the devil—whom Revelation calls "that old serpent"—will one day try to teach his
followers to practice human sacrifice on a wide scale as he
did when the Aztecs worshiped him as Quetzalcoatl, the
feathered serpent?

Opposition to Christianity

If the New Age movement is indeed going in the
direction I have suggested—toward more direct Satan
worship and more direct opposition to God—it seems that
we could expect to see evidences of this beginning to
appear in popular New Age writings today.

At first it amazed me when I discovered that this is
exactly what is happening. In materials I have written about
the New Age and in public presentations I have made, I
have always urged Christians to exercise restraint, compassion, and understanding toward those caught up in New
Age ideas. I have taken a particularly hard stand against
those alarmist Christians who have boosted sales of their
books by trying to prove that there is a humanly masterminded New Age conspiracy to destroy Christianity.

I still do not believe there is a centrally organized human
conspiracy against Christianity in the New Age movement.
But an alarming number of recently published New Age
books and magazine articles focus on the great harm that has
been done to our world through Western religion.

In order to understand how this is coming about, you
must first understand that the New Age movement has
become increasingly feminist through the years. In pointing this out, I must hasten to reiterate that just because
some members of a group are associated with the New

-ge movement does not necessarily mean the group's goals are New Age-oriented. Many women who are supportive of women's rights do not espouse New Age views.

New Age events I have attended typically draw about 70 percent women and 30 percent men. Recently in a magazine that gives mailing address lists that are available for sale to direct-mail advertisers, I saw a list advertised that was made up of people who had recently purchased New Age-oriented items. Significantly, the magazine noted that 70 percent of the people on the list were female.

Now, there is nothing wrong with the feminine rights movement in and of itself. Historically women have been given the short end of the stick in almost every society in which men have been dominant. But the way that some women go about seeking to overcome male dominance is both frightening and dangerous. Some, particularly those who have been abused by men, become involved in witchcraft to gain special powers over men. In fact, witchcraft is one of the entry paths that lead people into the New Age movement.

But even the feminists who do not take this radical step are beginning to speak more and more about the virtues of goddess worship and to teach that every woman is a goddess. Margot Adler pointed this out back in 1979 in her landmark book about modern witchcraft, *Drawing Down the Moon*: "Enter one of the many feminist bookstores in this country and look at the titles of poetry and literary magazines with names like *Hecate*, *13th Moon*, *Dragons and Gorgons*, *Hera*, *Wicce*, and *Sinister Wisdom*, and you will have an idea of the connection between witchcraft and goddess worship and the women's movement. Almost all these magazines identify women with the goddess and with witches." [26] Adler also points out that during the 1970s most of the feminist groups first became involved in consciousness raising (a New Age concept), and then in paganistic or witchcraft-oriented spirituality. [27] She herself became a witch (a term she does not use disparagingly).

In recent visits to New Age bookstores I have noticed that books on such topics as "The Goddess Within" are becoming more and more popular. On the surface this is no different from the general New Age teaching that we all are gods. But teaching about goddess worship has a further implication that comes out clearly in a recent book published by Harper and Row. *The Great Cosmic Mother* (a book that, significantly, has a picture on the cover of a feminine deity grasping nine serpents in her hand) is not only clearly anti-male, but also anti-Western religion. The gist of the authors' argument is that the original religion of humankind exalted women as gods and that it was only when Judaism introduced the story of the temptation in the Garden of Eden that men became the dominant force in religion and society.

Thus, the authors blame the Judaeo-Christian (and equally the Muslim) tradition for all the degradation and abuse women have suffered for the past several millennia, as well as for the wars that male aggressiveness has caused.* The frontispiece in the book takes issue with Michelangelo's Sistine Chapel rendering of Creation by picturing the Creation story under the title of "God Giving Birth"—a female goddess is pictured creating life via the normal channels of human reproduction.

To me it is fascinating to see that this attempt to discredit Judaeo-Christian religion in the eyes of feminine and feminist New Age devotees promotes the same old lie that every other branch of the New Age movement promotes about the nonexistence of a devil in Eden.

---

* Compare this to New Age channel Ruth Montgomery's assertion that the Age of Aquarius (New Age) will be more peaceful because of the declining influence of Christianity as we move out of the fish sign of Pisces into the sign of Aquarius. The fish was the earliest of Christian symbols, and Montgomery points out that the age of Pisces began just before the birth of Christ.

While there may not be a human conspiracy behind all this, it seems probable that all these facets are being marshaled together behind the scenes. And the most likely candidate for grand marshal of the parade to dethrone God and the truth He has revealed about the devil is—you guessed it—Lucifer himself. He's the one who has the most to gain by persuading people that he doesn't exist!

Why People Are Vulnerable

All Satan's strategies and machinations would be powerless if there was not a ready crop of people just waiting to be garnered in to his harvest of deceived souls.

A number of factors have created a situation that makes many people vulnerable to Satan's deception in our world today. Of course, in many parts of the world, religion has been dominated by demons for millennia. But what has opened the doors for the rapid growth of anti-Christian beliefs in America, the supposed bastion of Christianity?

There is not space here to repeat the story I related in *Secrets of the New Age* of the path of disillusionment with technology that has led to the youth counterculture of the sixties and on into the New Age movement. Suffice it to say for now that God has placed within all of us a need for spiritual nurture and contact with the supernatural. But by and large the churches of America have fallen into the trap of institutionalism and have been more concerned with preserving the status quo than with nurturing people spiritually. As a result, masses of people have become disillusioned with traditional religion and have gone seeking to satisfy their spiritual drives elsewhere.

Add to this the libertarian, individualistic ideals that dominate American thought, and you get a large group of people whose needs have not been met by religion and who cannot abide the restrictiveness of most religious creeds, yet who are looking for a spiritual experience. Unwilling to accept God's law, they seek spiritual enlightenment in ways that will not restrict their free lifestyle.

The stories of the many channels who first rejected God, then came into contact with another supernatural spirit that denies the Bible and the existence of Satan, illustrate that Satan is just waiting to step in and fill the spiritual void in the life of anyone who rejects God.

To put it bluntly, many people fall prey to the deceptions of the New Age movement because they have rejected God's truth. In chapter 10 I'll have more to say about the tragic results prophesied for those who reject truth. But in chapter 8 we need to look at some further evidences of where New Age philosophy is taking its believers—and why. In chapter 9 I will draw together the evidence we have looked at so far to gain additional insight into the reason that the New Age movement is leading us in the direction it is.

CHAPTER

8

The Longing
Look Back

On November 19, 1989, Pastor Sylvester Case turned his car off of State Highway 44 in New Mexico and headed off across the desert on a dirt road whose surface often resembled a washboard. People had told us to expect the 29-mile trip to Chaco Canyon to take at least an hour because of the condition of the road.

I had come to New Mexico chiefly to speak in Pastor Case's church in Farmington about the New Age movement. He had invited me because he knew there was a lot of interest in New Age things in his area. Shortly before my trip I learned that there had been a large New Age gathering in Chaco Canyon during the Harmonic Convergence in 1987. So when I discovered that the road to the canyon lay right along the way between Albuquerque and Farmington, I persuaded the good pastor to make a little detour on the trip back to the airport.

I wasn't nearly as sure why I should make this trip as I had been about the purpose of my trip to Cerro de las Estrellas. I knew that I would find the remains of an ancient Indian civilization, but I wasn't at all sure why the New Age devotees had selected it as one of the "power points" for their convergence.

After nearly an hour of bumping along on the ill-maintained road, we arrived at a sign that announced our entrance into Chaco Canyon National Historical Park. It was a relief to pull onto the park's paved roadway. Noticing a parking area, we pulled off the road to investigate. A sign indicated that we were at Casa Rinconada, a settlement area that includes the largest kiva in the park. The Anasazi Indians, who settled this area more than 1,000 years ago, built their villages around large circular buildings called kivas, which they apparently used for religious ceremonies. The kiva at Casa Rinconada proved to be about 70 feet across and had several altarlike structures inside.

Continuing up the road, we soon came to the park's visitor center, and I struck up a conversation with the lone National Park Service ranger behind the counter. I asked him about the Harmonic Convergence, and he told me that there had been nearly 5,000 people camped out in the park for the celebration. "And how many sites are there in the campground?" I asked.

"Only 40 in the regular campground," he replied. "But we set up a special camping area just for that group."

"What site were they most interested in?"

"Mainly in Casa Rinconada, but a few other sites, too."

That meant that I had already seen the most important New Age site in the park. But I couldn't for the life of me figure out what made that round structure so important.

A tour through the center's museum didn't do much to answer my questions either. All I learned was that the Anasazi had for the most part abandoned Chaco Canyon before the Europeans came and that they had taken with them most of their possessions, leaving behind few artifacts that could yield significant information about their lifestyle or religion. Books about the area didn't yield any more answers. I knew that the Harmonic Convergence's promoters had selected many power points throughout the world. But why they had chosen this little-understood site remained a mystery.

Mysteries are not uncommon in the New Age movement. People I have talked to at New Age gatherings often don't know a lot about the basis of the movement, but they are attracted to it nonetheless. So it wouldn't surprise me to learn that most of the people who gathered at the Harmonic Convergence came for the experience rather than because of a real understanding of the significance of the power points or the celebration. Certainly there could not be a very cogent argument for the gathering here in a canyon whose religious history is lost in the mists of time.

Connecting With the Past

My visit to the site of the Harmonic Convergence in Chaco Canyon brought to mind a different type of New Age gathering that I attended in 1988. The Natural Living Expo, held in the National Guard Armory in Silver Spring, Maryland, was jointly sponsored by one of the Washington, D.C., area's largest New Age organizations and the publishers of the most important New Age tabloid in the nation's capital.

Wandering the aisles of displays that filled the auditorium level, I met psychics, channels, shamans, shiatsu practitioners, masseuses, aura readers, witches, fortune-tellers, crystal sellers, spiritual guides, numerologists, and a host of other New Age professionals who had found a way to capitalize on people's renewed interest in holistic health and ancient earth religions.

Many of the people who were displaying their arts and wares for sale in the auditorium were also scheduled to teach classes on the lower level of the armory. I attended a number of these classes, but didn't find any of them particularly enlightening. Many of the lecturers and their listeners seemed content to rely on hearsay and what they called "channeled information" as adequate references to support their beliefs.

I was particularly amazed and amused at the presentation given by a woman who bills herself as Washington, D.C.'s crystal lady. She began her lecture by telling us that her credentials as an expert on crystals consisted chiefly of having had a relative who was a geologist and having spent the past seven years experimenting with and selling crystals.

About 170 people had crowded into the lecture room, filling all but the back rows of folding chairs. "How many of you are somewhat familiar with what crystals can do for you?" she asked. Almost everyone raised a hand. "How many of you have experimented with crystals yourself?" I was almost alone in not raising my hand. I didn't figure that my boyhood experience of growing salt crystals in a jar was the type of thing she was talking about.

Amazed at how many people were already working with crystals, seeking special powers from them, I began scrutinizing those who had gathered in the room. There were hardly any far-out types. In fact, most of the people there looked like yuppies. Not surprisingly, though, in light of the statistics I shared earlier, the preponderance of participants were female.

My knowledge of crystals up to this point was limited to what I had read in books and catalogs and had seen at displays in New Age-oriented stores, so I was most interested to find out what the crystal lady herself would have to say.

To say the least, I was disappointed. Not a shred of credible evidence for the value of crystals in health, healing, or prosperity did she present. Instead, she contented herself with assertions. She assured us, for example, that clear quartz crystals are extremely valuable for their absorptive properties. They can absorb both good and bad vibrations. "So it would be good to have a supply of them in your office at work," she explained. They would prove especially helpful on days when the boss comes in and really bawls you out for something. The crystals would, she claimed, absorb all the bad vibrations from the boss's negativity and take them out of the environment.

She went on to give instructions for clearing the crystals of the bad influences they had absorbed. The proper procedure, she said, was to turn them point down and take them to a sink. After saying a little prayer (she didn't indicate to whom the prayer should be addressed, but other things she said led me to believe the recipient must be some great spirit in the sky; anyhow, I felt certain that it wasn't to the God who has revealed Himself in the Bible) to ask that the negative vibrations be turned into something positive so that they wouldn't hurt anyone else, one should run tap water over the crystal and let the vibrations go down the drain!

Further tidbits of "wisdom" I picked up from the crystal lady included an explanation of why there is no unanimity (let alone harmony) of opinion among crystal touters as to which crystals will work for which purposes. These discrepancies come about because all the information on crystals' value is coming from channeled sources (and the implication is that you can't expect channels to agree about things). There is general agreement that crystals resonate with the various bodily chakras, according to the frequency of the visible light they reflect (Eastern philosophy teaches that the body has seven chakras ranging in color from red at the base of the spine to violet at the top of the head). But since different sources prescribe different crystals for different purposes, the best way to find out what works, according to the crystal lady, is to acquire a wide variety of crystals and experiment with them yourself. The best rule of thumb, then, is: Whatever works for you works for you! The key is to have plenty of crystals of different colors to experiment with.

Immediately after her presentation, the crystal lady hurried up to the main auditorium, where the staff at her crystal sales booth was having difficulty coping with the throng of people waiting for counsel on which crystals to buy!

I found myself simply shaking my head in amazement that, after such an illogical, blatantly sales-oriented presentation, apparently well-educated people would rush to fulfill the hopes of the saleslady. Clearly the days of the patent medicine salesman are not past. Other presentations at the same conference confirmed my observation. Patent medicines no longer need be ~~sold~~ by traveling salesmen who leave town as soon as they've dispensed their nostrums. New Age fascination with ancient arts has opened a vast, new, prosperous market for their cure-alls.

Later in the day I encountered one of the organizers of the Natural Living Expo, a man whom I considered a close enough friend to level with. He had told me previously that his interest in New Age things had come about mainly through help he had gotten with a health problem and that he didn't give much credence to what he called the airy-fairy elements of the movement. So I shared my honest impressions of the crystal lady's presentation. "It was the stupidest thing I have ever heard," I confessed. He seemed a bit surprised, but not offended. A few moments later, though, I noticed that his wife, an intelligent, attractive woman in her 30s, was wearing a quartz crystal pendant necklace.

Oh, well . . . so much for my expertise in how to win friends and influence people!

Seriously, though, I've shared these two stories as illustrations of where the New Age movement is coming from. It draws many of its devotees from among the well-educated people of Western society whose disillusionment with traditional Western values leads them to be open to almost any alternative that presents itself.

The *New Age Catalog*, published in 1988, lists books and other products from scores of New Age-oriented disciplines ranging from crystal healing through iridology, reflexology, homeopathy, rolfing, acupuncture, and acupressure to books detailing the recondite "readings" Edgar Cayce gave while in a trance. New Age tabloids I have picked up in different parts of the country confirm my assessment. Alternate therapies attract millions of New Age dollars whether or not there is any sound basis for their practice.

Articles in the secular press marvel at the epidemic of gullibility that has swept millions into belief in almost any esoteric school of thought that presents itself. In a fascinating interview with David Spangler, author of *Revelation: The Birth of a New Age* and one of the most important early proponents of New Age thought, I learned that even he did not have much respect for many of the influences that come under the New Age term these days. So I asked whom he considered to be representative of true New Age thought. One of the people he mentioned was Ken Wilber, a man whose name I had come upon quite often in researching the movement. Imagine my surprise, then, to discover Wilber's current reaction to the New Age movement. His definition, along with other positive and negative assessments, was printed in the October 1987 issue of *Omni* magazine. According to Wilber, the New Age movement is "California-holographic-bleached-brain garbage. The baby boomers who produced the New Age were the first television generation. They got steered into immediate gratification. You don't like channel 2, switch. Channel 5, switch. And so on. We have the highest divorce rate in history. We have the most difficult time forming lasting, stable relationships. We're instant gratification. Don't like present reality? Switch. New Age. Pow!" (p. 162).

Spangler also told me that he had recently viewed a television debate between a purported New Age channel and a fundamentalist Christian, and had found himself rooting for the Christian because of the silliness of the channel. [28] But recent news reports reveal that this channel continues to attract a large following. Many of her believers have gone so far as to sell their homes, pull up roots, and move to the West Coast town where she lives.

The current New Age fascination with channeling is just one more evidence that the movement is taking a longing look back to more primitive religions. As I pointed out in *Secrets of the New Age,* channeling is just a modern manifestation of the old art of shamanism that has been practiced in traditional cultures around the world. But there is real danger in these adventures with guides from unknown realms. Some within the movement are beginning to recognize this, but others continue to seek direct communication with Satan and his deceptive spirits.

Wilber and Spangler are not alone in becoming disillusioned with what the New Age movement has become since it became big news and big business. But those who continue their gallop in search of the latest fad far outnumber the more seasoned observers who have discovered that all that glitters with New Age promises is not gold.

What Makes People Gullible

If gullibility is a hallmark of many who pursue the New Age, the question is What has made them this way? And a second, more important question is How far can they be led? If Satan's real goal in leading people is to get them to do things that will hurt God, and if people are opening themselves up to be led by Satan, what will the ultimate outcome be for you? for me? Will it lead to war, murder, sacrifice?

The second question and those following it will be the focus of chapters 9-11. In my own consideration of the first question I have found several Bible verses particularly helpful.

New Testament scholars recognize that one of the apostle Paul's chief concerns in his Epistles was to combat the influence of Gnosticism in the early Christian church. Since ideas from ancient Gnosticism play a prominent part in some people's pursuit of the New Age, what Paul wrote nearly 2,000 years ago is relevant today to people who are looking to long-outmoded thought patterns for what they consider to be new enlightenment.

In Ephesians 4:17-19 Paul points his finger squarely at the source of the problems the non-Christians in his world were experiencing, and he cautions his Christian friends against falling into the same trap. In the verses that follow he goes on to remind his friends of how Christ can make their lives much better than they were before they became Christians.

"This I say, therefore, and testify in the Lord, that you should no longer walk as the rest of the Gentiles walk, in the futility of their mind, having their understanding darkened, being alienated from the life of God, because of the ignorance that is in them, because of the hardening of their heart; who, being past feeling, have given themselves over to licentiousness, to work all uncleanness with greediness" (NKJV).

I find this text especially relevant to the New Age movement because of the movement's emphasis on development of human potential through full use of the powers of the mind. Paul looks at people's enthusiasm for human potential and calls it what it is—the futility of their mind.

Despite the stupendous advances in communication, data storage and retrieval, computer science, and instruments for the study of natural phenomena, we are still up against the limitations of the human mind. We are unable to perceive, let alone fully understand, everything that happens around us. The best educated among us have had to specialize in such a narrow field of research that we sometimes cannot see the broader picture.

To Paul the reason for the non-Christians' lack of understanding is their alienation from the life of God, which has been offered freely to them, but which they either have not heard about or have rejected. At the end of verse 18 he implies that it is their own fault "because of the hardening of their heart."

He then goes on to describe the results of this hardening. Having lost the ability to experience normal emotions, they give themselves over to the stronger compulsions of lust and licentiousness (cf. verse 22). To Paul the cause of ignorance and gullibility is simple. It comes from separation from God, the source of wisdom.

Is it possible, then, that what we see, particularly in the less rational branches of the New Age movement, is just the natural outworking of people's attempts to save themselves, or at least to prosper without God's help?

If it weren't for evidences of the supernatural in the movement, this might be a safe assumption. But many of those who have cut themselves off from God have tapped into another supernatural source of power and spirituality.

Is it Satan who is behind all of this? Whose is the face behind the mask? To this question we must turn in the next chapter.

CHAPTER

9

The Face
Behind the Mask

By this you know the Spirit of God: Every spirit that confesses that Jesus Christ has come in the flesh is of God, and every spirit that does not confess that Jesus Christ has come in the flesh is not of God. And this is the spirit of the Antichrist, which you have heard was coming, and is now already in the world" (1 John 4:2, 3, NKJV).

For many years I puzzled over this text. In a way I almost wished it weren't in the Bible! Because it seemed too obvious. Or rather it seemed to give Satan and the antichrist too obvious a way to deceive Christians. All Satan would have to do, I thought, would be to start inspiring his prophets to confess that Jesus Christ had indeed come in the flesh, then lead those who listened to this message from the false prophet off on another tangent of error. Even the antichrist himself would simply have to make a pretense of confessing this, and then he could lead people into whatever other error he pleased.

It seemed such an obvious strategy. I couldn't imagine that Satan would ever again inspire any false prophet without also sending along through that false prophet the message that Jesus Christ had come in the flesh. But I hadn't reckoned with Satan's enmity against Jesus Christ.

I hadn't realized just how hard it would be for Satan to admit that the Lord of the universe had condescended to live for more than 30 years in human flesh and then to allow people to mock Him, scourge Him, spit on Him, and finally nail Him to the cruel torture instrument known as a cross.

Such a confession sticks in Satan's craw, and he just won't speak it or inspire anyone else to. Because if he admits that, he also has to admit that he was the tempter who tried to sidetrack Jesus from His mission. And he has to admit that he is the one who took over people's lives in the demon possession stories related in the Gospels and that he is the one whose evil spirits Jesus overcame and cast out.

But I didn't realize this, so it came as a real surprise when I discovered that every New Age prophet, psychic, and channel who claims inspiration from a supernatural spirit flat out denies that Jesus Christ has come in the flesh.

Sir George and the Christ Spirit

With a little help from the Ayatollah Khomeini I was able to get an interview with one of the most fascinating New Age leaders I have ever met. Sir George Trevelyan is known as the father of adult education in England, and he is also widely known as the father of the New Age movement there. I had seen his name often in books and articles about the movement, and had read his book *A Vision of the Aquarian Age*. So when I arrived at the Heart to Heart Festival in Washington, D.C., in February of 1989 and discovered that he was there too, I determined to get an interview with him.

Sir George is in his 80s and is a bit hard of hearing, but mentally is as sharp as a tack. In conversation he never misses a beat and never permits himself to ramble off and forget what he originally intended to say. When I approached him, I introduced myself as an editor from *Ministry*, an international journal read by clergy of various denominations all over the world, and told him that I was researching the relationship between the New Age movement and Christianity.

He assured me that this was a topic of great interest to him and said that he would be glad to grant an interview if it could be worked into his schedule. Unfortunately, though, he had a very busy schedule and would be heading back to England in just a few days.

We weren't able to get together for the interview at the festival, so the next day I contacted the organization that had sponsored it and asked if they could set up a time for me to interview him. The secretary I spoke with did her best to arrange a time for an interview, but despite her best efforts, Sir George left for the airport before I could work into his schedule.

But I got the interview anyhow—and this is where I like to say I got a little help from Khomeini. It was during the time of the Muslim world's great furor over the book *Satanic Verses*, by Salman Rushdie, and Khomeini had issued a death threat, offering a reward to anyone who would kill Rushdie. I'm not sure exactly what happened in relation to that crisis, but it all worked out well for me because a threat from Khomeini closed London's Heathrow Airport, and Sir George had to stay in Washington, D.C. for another day. The secretary called to say that if I would come over right away, I could have my interview.

Dropping everything, I hurried immediately to the organization's headquarters in Chevy Chase, Maryland. In the course of our interview I learned that Sir George was raised in a prestigious British family and that his grandfather was an agnostic and his father an atheist. So he had virtually no religious instruction as a boy and manifested no interest in spiritual things until the day during World War II that he describes as the most important day of his life. He spent that day in Scotland, where he had gone to learn about organic gardening. While he was there, the people who were teaching him about gardening persuaded him to listen to a lecture about the basis of their philosophy. These persons were followers of Rudolph Steiner, who broke off from the Theosophical Society to found the Anthroposophical Society in 1912.

Sir George told me that the hour he spent listening to the presentation about anthroposophy was the most important hour of his life, for it was then that he came to understand that there are angels and other supernatural beings in our universe.

I soon discovered, though, that his understanding of angels, and particularly of Christ, was very different from what the Bible teaches. In particular, when I asked him about his understanding of Christ, he confirmed what I should have expected. Sir George believes that Jesus was just a normal human being up to the time of His baptism and that at His baptism a spirit descended on Him and He became, for a limited time, the embodiment of this spirit, who had descended on other great prophets, such as Abraham, Moses, and Buddha before Him. And that furthermore, this spirit left Jesus' body at the time of the Crucifixion.

This view of Christ's nature is, with a few variations, an almost universal New Age doctrine. It seems only a slight modification of the Christian viewpoint, and New Age leaders believe that Christians should be able to come into harmony with this view.

What they don't realize is that this doctrine denies the most important elements of Christianity and that it falls into the category of antichrist doctrine when it is put to the test of 1 John 4.

If Jesus were just a normal human being who consented to allow His body to be used temporarily by a spirit who could come and go at will, then God did not do anything unique in Him. In fact, God did not suffer at all for the salvation of His world, but simply sent a spirit of wisdom to give us good advice about how to live our lives.

The glory of the gospel message is that the very same God who created this world and gave its inhabitants the power of choice was willing to come and suffer the consequences of His created beings' wrong choices. The fullness of God's love and justice becomes truly evident only when we realize this.

God is not some detached essence of omnipotence sitting on a throne somewhere, untouched by the sorrow and woe that have come about because He decided to give Adam and Eve the right to decide to obey or disobey Him. No! The gospel proclaims that "in the beginning was the Word, and the Word was with God, and the Word was God. He was in the beginning with God. All things were made through Him, and without Him nothing was made that was made. . . . And the Word became flesh and dwelt among us" (John 1:1-14, NKJV). Jesus was and is the Lord and Creator of the universe. And it was He, not some human receptacle of a transient spirit, who took upon Himself the consequences of all the bad choices that have been made since He gave us the power to make choices!

But Satan will do anything he can to keep people from realizing the great love Jesus manifested by coming to share our suffering and sorrow. That is why I no longer worry about 1 John 4. Its warning is safe from satanic interdiction. For even though Satan would like very much to lead people astray, he cannot bring himself to confess or proclaim that Jesus Christ has indeed come in the flesh and dwelt among us as God Himself. So none of the prophets or antichrists he sends will ever wiggle around the warning in this text.

Discovering the Mask

Leaders of the New Age movement with whom I have spoken typically affirm that their belief system does not in any way run contrary to Christianity—or at least that nothing in Christianity countermands acceptance of New Age ideas. If they believed otherwise, they would not have accepted me so warmly and openly.

But if they understood even the most basic of Christian doctrines, they would realize that they have been deceived. One cannot believe that Jesus was a mere human, without denying the Bible's account of His incarnation, life, death, and resurrection.

And if they are deceived on this most basic of doctrines, what about the rest of what they teach? If it is not founded on directly channeled Satanic inspiration, chances are good that it is founded on what Paul calls the "futility of their mind" (Ephesians 4:17).

But the incredible thing that I have discovered, as I have studied the various philosophies and religions—New Age and others—that are captivating people's minds today, is the unanimity with which they agree on the very point that John pointed out as being symptomatic of the antichrist's position. Even among Christians we can observe a weakening of belief that the same God who created us came to live among us and redeem us. To start with, many who call themselves Christians today don't even believe that the Genesis account of Creation is true. [29] Others tend to think of Christ as merely a good teacher and example.

In my early research on the New Age movement, I began to search for reasons that the movement's followers so strongly preferred Eastern religion and ancient pagan religions to Christianity. I thought it might be just a desire for something different. But my recent research has turned up a mounting pile of evidence that the movement is progressing beyond the point of experimentation and is casting about to find a religious framework on which to build. By and large the framework has already been selected, and it consists of almost any sort of religion that does not require belief in any absolute, such as a once-and-for-all-time in-the-flesh revelation of God in the Man Christ Jesus.

But because religion without the supernatural is just powerless philosophy, those who become involved with non-Christian thought systems often become open to messages received through channeling.

Rejecting Christ

What is happening now is that people who have rejected Christianity but still want contact with the supernatural are joining the New Age movement through such diverse paths as witchcraft, polytheism, paganism, and goddess worship. Others who do not feel a compelling need for supernatural elements in their lives are accepting New Age philosophy without the channeled elements. Thus many may choose to believe simply that our spirits have evolved through the millennia to a state in which we are ready to make an evolutionary jump into a higher realm that will constitute the New Age. Some of these may see the sources of channels' information as purely natural manifestations of communication with people from earth or elsewhere who have already evolved to a higher plane.

But whatever angle people take, and whether or not they accept New Age ideas, if they reject Christ they are open to the deceptions of the antichrist.

Many times I tell audiences that invite me to speak about the New Age movement that the movement is not the real danger to Christians in our world today. In fact, it is just one among many movements afoot to destroy faith in God's provision of salvation in Jesus. Most Christians are more likely to be swept away by relativism or secularism or materialism than by New Ageism. And the danger is heightened by putting too much emphasis on the New Age movement. Because while we are spending all our energy keeping track of what the channels and crystal salesmen are doing, Satan just may sneak in the back door and catch us with some other hook that doesn't as blatantly deny Christ's first advent, but just as effectively destroys our faith in the one Saviour whom God has provided.

Once Christians abandon faith in Christ and begin to look to themselves for salvation, Satan doesn't care whether they turn within and become New Age channels or simply begin to rely on the works of their own hands to provide for the present and future. The results are the same. He has rent them away from God, and they are defenseless against his devilish deceptions.

Historically those religions that have not known of or have rejected God's provision for salvation through His Son have almost without exception turned to human sacrifice as a means to save themselves. (Buddhism is an exception, but it really is the product of a reform movement within Hinduism, which practiced sacrifice. And in a sense Buddhism's emphasis on renouncement of life and normal human aspirations is a nonbloody form of human sacrifice. The Japanese kamikaze pilots of World War II found the courage for their sacrifice in this renouncement.) It is as though we know in our inmost selves that we cannot really save ourselves and that we need someone else to give his or her life in our place. An unmitigated sense of unworthiness plagues our souls. We know we need a Saviour.

God has provided a Saviour. But many find it distasteful to accept the provision, and so they seek another that, rather than relying wholly on the mercy of God, gives self a part in achieving salvation. Even the Jewish Pharisees of Jesus' day had this problem. Of them the apostle Paul wrote: "They being ignorant of God's righteousness, and seeking to establish their own righteousness, have not submitted to the righteousness of God" (Romans 10:3, NKJV).

And it is one of the best known facts of history that these Pharisees resorted to something very like human sacrifice when they saw their self-centered system of salvation threatened by One whom they considered a mere itinerant troublemaker from Galilee. "Then the chief priests and the Pharisees gathered a council and said, 'What shall we do? For this Man works many signs. If we let Him alone like this, everyone will believe in Him, and the Romans will come and take away both our place and nation.' And one of them, Caiaphas, being high priest that year, said to them, 'You know nothing at all, nor do you consider that it is expedient for us that one man should die for the people, and not that the whole nation should perish' " (John 11:47-50, NKJV). The similarity between this rationale and what I see as the Aztecs' reasons for extracting human hearts is too obvious to ignore. What happened on the cross was not human sacrifice per se. But its motivation—and the motivator behind it—were the same.

The point is that one need not believe in New Age channels, join a witches' coven, or even openly deny Christ, to be prepared to be led astray by the antichrist. One need only abandon faith in the once-and-for-all-time provision of God for the salvation of His world. Everyone who falls into this trap is ready and waiting to follow the antichrist either wittingly or unwittingly.

How and where Satan will lead his followers is the topic of the next two chapters.

CHAPTER
10

The Prophecies Foretell It

We have reviewed a lot of evidence. We have seen that religious cults under the guidance of Satan have throughout history and in every part of the world turned to human sacrifice in an attempt to work out their own salvation. We have seen that even well-educated, supposedly civilized people today can be led by Satan to practice human sacrifice. And we have seen clear evidence that many groups within the New Age movement not only leave themselves open to Luciferic guidance but also actively invite his intervention in their lives through witchcraft, shamanism, and channeling. We have noted that the New Age emphasis on reincarnation and monism leads to the devaluation of individual human life and that other movements and influences in society are also tending toward this devaluation.

But it still seems a bit farfetched to predict that human sacrifice may return as an accepted part of life in the mainstream. Unless you really understand history and are willing to recognize that none of its wars could have been fought if the aggressors who started each war had not been willing to sacrifice others' lives for their own gain. Unless you can hear an echo of human sacrifice in the death sentences that rang through the German stalags and concentration camps. Unless you can recognize, in the philosophy of the officials who condemned prisoners to what Alexander Solzhenitzyn calls the Gulag Archipelago, the age-old message that the few must suffer for the betterment of the masses. Unless you can read in the eyes of the Chinese Red Brigadists, and Pol Pot, and the Ayatollah Khomeini, and the leaders of the Irish Republican Army, and the hit men of the Colombian drug cartels, and the pistol-packing preteen in Los Angeles that same message that it doesn't matter if someone else dies, just as long as it means I can survive and prosper. Unless, in short, you realize that it is basic to human nature to preserve oneself at the expense of others. And unless you realize that Satan has been an expert at honing this basic human characteristic to a dagger point ever since he used it so effectively to ensnare Cain and destroy Abel.

Some would argue that the killings I have listed above do not fit under the heading of human sacrifice because they are not religiously motivated attempts at appeasing or pleasing a god. But in the religion that motivates what I believe is modern-day human sacrifice, self is the god. Just as it is in New Age doctrine. And in all these Satan is the piper who plays the tune the killers march to. He doesn't care whether people are killed by drug runners or overt satanists. His goal is to devalue human life to the point where people are killed and the killer's respect for God's ultimate creation is destroyed.

The Five Prongs of the New Age Movement

Satan has given a five-pronged strategy to the New Age movement to help break down Western society's barriers against human sacrifice.

The first prong teaches people that there is really no

such thing as good and evil—that there is only one force that has both light and dark sides.

The second prong pokes into our recognition of our inherently evil, selfish nature by persuading people that inside themselves they are naturally filled with and controlled by the light side of the force. People who accept this lie are oblivious to their need of God's grace to change them and unaware that unless they are changed at the core they will readily agree to sacrificing anyone who appears to be obstructing their path to success or whose survival might compromise their own prosperity.

The third prong breaks down people's resistance to following Satan's direct guidance by teaching them that the path to true enlightenment is to turn within and seek spirit guides. Satan can speak to New Age channels just as well as he can to satanists whom he has already taught to practice human sacrifice.

The fourth prong tampers with our understanding of the significance of life by leading people to believe that each person's current body is just one in a long series of incarnations. Human sacrifice can be a natural outgrowth of this belief system because it is only natural that a person who is perceived to be bogged down in a wrong belief system in this life ought to be "liberated" and allowed to take on a new body in which he or she may be better able to achieve "enlightenment."

The fifth prong points people back to the ancient nature religions—many of which included human sacrifice—as more natural and beneficial than Christianity for humans in general, women in particular, and the ecology of our planet.

But does this necessarily mean that we can expect human sacrifice to become popular again?

Prophecy and the Future

It is always risky to try predicting the future. Even trying to interpret Bible prophecies to establish specific details is a bit dicey. More than one ship of faith has run aground and sunk on the reefs of misinterpreted prophecy. It is far safer to take prophecy as a guide to help us anticipate broad trends and as a kind of after-the-fact road map to reaffirm our faith that through it all God was in control and will continue to be in control.

In fact, Jesus affirmed this after-the-fact map effect as His chief reason for giving predictions to His disciples. In John 13:19 we read that He said to them, "Now I tell you before it comes, that when it does come to pass, you may believe that I am He" (NKJV). Compare His similar statements in John 14:29 and 16:4.

Having said that, I still must go on to say that it seems to me that current events and the movements we see gaining strength in the world form a highly significant confluence with the stream of Bible prophecies concerning the time just before the second coming of Jesus.

Even before the New Age paradigm shift began to change people's thinking about good and evil, we could see certain aspects of Paul's predictions recorded in 2 Timothy 3:1-9 coming to pass. Excerpts from that passage that describe how people will behave in the last days seem apt descriptions of our age: "Men shall be lovers of their own selves . . . lovers of pleasures more than lovers of God; having a form of godliness, but denying the power thereof. . . . Ever learning, and never able to come to the knowledge of the truth."

New Age doctrines give new life to old pagan ways of life. And what's more, the New Age has now brought false Christs and false prophets marching in droves onto the scene and into the popular consciousness—a development that would have been unthinkable only a few years ago when people tended to have more faith in science and technology and felt less of a need for the supernatural.

This seems to fulfill the first half of Matthew 24:24, a prophecy of events to take place just before the end of time and Christ's second coming: "For false christs and false prophets will arise." But the second half of this verse has not come to full fruition: "and show great signs and wonders, so as to deceive, if possible, even the elect" (NKJV).

The false christs and prophets have done some signs and wonders. There have been a few healings and just enough accurate predictions sprinkled amid the mass of confused prophetic speculations to maintain the faith of those who really want to believe. But there hasn't yet been anything startling and spectacular enough to come close to deceiving God's elect—those who will ultimately be redeemed from the earth (see verses 22, 31). Matthew 24:24 implies that these special people of God will not be deceived, but that the power of the signs worked by the false christs and prophets will be so great that it will nearly deceive them. It is clear, then, that everyone will be deceived except these very special people who will ultimately be caught up to Christ at His second coming. Elsewhere Jesus makes it clear that many people who consider themselves Christians are not really among this elect group (see Matthew 7:22, 23; John 15:5, 6). No doubt many of these supposed Christians will be deceived by the signs that lead so many astray.

Nothing the New Age movement or its christs and prophets has produced thus far has had such an alluring effect on the world. In fact, although the movement's popularity is growing among some, most people I mention it to in casual conversation are either unaware of it or have almost no idea what it is. (Which is not to say that the movement's philosophy has not altered their thinking—many have bought into New Age ideas without realizing where the ideas came from.)

And the Christian reaction to the New Age movement up to this point has been more of a setback than a victory for Satan's strategy of deception. Books by the bushel are pouring from Christian presses, warning against the seductiveness of the New Age movement. These books are being read widely, and their authors are invited to address large convocations of Christians.

So as far as Satan's forces making progress toward achieving a deception that will lead astray all but the elect, the New Age movement seems almost counterproductive. Right now it isn't even making strong inroads among nominal Christians (although some New Age teachings have been accepted by certain Christian groups). After reading New Age books and interviewing many New Age believers, I have concluded that most of the movement's converts come from among those who have basically rejected Christianity before becoming aware of New Age ideas.

What, then, could be the deeper, stronger deception that Jesus foresaw? I believe it will be the product of the coming together of New Ageism with other important movements that are gaining strength today. Two other important Bible prophecies help me understand how this could come about.

The Last Great Deception

In His discussion of the end of time, Jesus stopped short of disclosing just exactly what great signs and wonders would sway those in the church who are not so firmly rooted that they cannot be moved. However, after His ascension Jesus revealed the details of this deception to the apostles Paul and John.

John gives us our first glimpse of what is to happen in the final days before Jesus returns to put an end to history as we know it and to establish His eternal kingdom: "Little children, it is the last hour; and as you have heard that the antichrist is coming, even now many antichrists have come, by which we know that it is the last hour" (1 John 2:18, NKJV; see also 4:1-3; 2 John 7). Throughout his Epistles John makes a clear distinction between the many antichrists who were already active and could be recognized by their denial that Jesus Christ had come in the flesh and the one antichrist whose spirit was already present in the antichrists, but who was yet to come in the flesh.

The apostle Paul developed the same theme but in different terms in his second letter to the church at Thessalonica. Concerning the day of the Lord—the day of Christ's return—he wrote: "Let no one deceive you by any means; for that Day will not come unless the falling away comes first, and the man of sin is revealed, the son of perdition" (2 Thessalonians 2:3, NKJV).

Two things are especially important in this verse. First of all, it points out that Paul, like John, expects one specific "man of sin"—antichrist—to make his appearance at the end of time.

The second important point is that Paul expects there to be a "falling away" during this same end-time period. This falling away is the same phenomenon that Jesus spoke of when He implied that all but the very elect would be deceived and led astray by the deceptive signs and wonders.

John spoke of a similar phenomenon when he divulged the information that the antichrists who were active in his day had once been a part of the church: "They went out from us, but they were not of us; for if they had been of us, they would have continued with us" (1 John 2:19, NKJV).

So both Paul and John expected a specific antichrist to come and lead astray all but the elect in the last days. John pointed out that this was already happening on a small scale. Paul continued his warning with this startling passage: "The coming of the lawless one is according to the working of Satan, with all power, signs, and lying wonders, and with all unrighteous deception among those who perish, because they did not receive the love of the truth, that they might be saved. And for this reason God will send them strong delusion, that they should believe the lie, that they all may be condemned who did not believe the truth but had pleasure in unrighteousness" (2 Thessalonians 2:9-12, NKJV).

Here he reveals that everyone—church members and nonmembers alike—who fails to learn to love (not just accept) God's truth and who continues to take pleasure in unrighteousness will be deceived by the antichrist with a delusion straight from God Himself! Paul said it; I didn't: "God will send them strong delusion."

I wouldn't know what to make of this passage if it weren't for another message that Jesus sent to John near the end of John's long life. This message, recorded in Revelation 13, puts flesh on the skeleton outline of end-time events that Paul gives in 2 Thessalonians.

In Revelation 13 John writes about the antichrist under the symbol of a beast that "deceives those who dwell on the earth by those signs which he was granted to do" (verse 14, NKJV). If we link up this verse with the passage from 2 Thessalonians, it seems clear that it is God Himself who grants this particular beast the power to do these signs.

Fire From Heaven

Chief among the signs used to deceive people is that "he even makes fire come down from heaven on the earth in the sight of men" (verse 13, NKJV). Because we have been discussing human sacrifice, it is important to note here that fire from heaven is usually associated with sacrifice of some sort.

This certainly is an amazing and significant sign. Historically God has reserved the power to call down fire from heaven for Himself and His own prophets. God Himself did it in the case of Sodom and Gomorrah (Genesis 19:24). God also sent a miraculous fire onto the altar of burnt offering in the presence of Moses and Aaron (Leviticus 9:23, 24). And fire once again came forth from God as punishment upon the disobedient priests Nadab and Abihu (Leviticus 10:1, 2).

But the most famous instance of fire falling from heaven to earth is described in 1 Kings 18. In that well-known incident the prophet Elijah set up a test before the people of Israel to prove whom they should worship—Baal, the reputed carrier of lightning, or Yahweh, the God who had revealed Himself to Abraham and Moses, and who had led Israel out of captivity in Egypt.

Elijah challenged the prophets of Baal to try to call fire down from heaven. When they failed, Elijah had the Lord's altar soaked with water, and then he prayed a simple prayer. Instantly "the fire of the Lord fell and consumed the burnt sacrifice, and the wood and the stones and the dust, and it licked up the water that was in the trench" (1 Kings 18:38, NKJV).

This is the case in point that makes the sign of Revelation 13 important. For the ability to call down fire from heaven has always been a sign that God reserved for Himself. Almost every Christian—and Jew and Muslim—

knows that. So when God allows the antichrist beast to perform this sign, many who have become Christians but have never learned to really love God's truth and to dig into His Word and treasure it above all else will be deceived. Thinking they are worshiping the God of Moses and Elijah, they will end up bowing down to the antichrist!

But what does all this have to do with reinstituting and popularizing human sacrifice?

The link is not obvious unless you understand the basis on which Satan has typically persuaded people to begin sacrificing human beings (see chapter 3). When the Aztecs sacrificed 20,000 victims a year, it was to feed and give strength to the gods they worshiped. One of the most important of their rituals was the New Fire ceremony, in which once every 52 years they had to extinguish all of their fires and rekindle a new fire. They kindled this new fire on the chest of a human victim whose life was sacrificed to give strength to the sun. We noted in chapter 5 that some in the New Age movement are already calling the earth a goddess under the name Gaia and that others are calling for a return to polytheism. Is it possible that the sun may also be returned to god status sometime soon? A conversation I had with a devout Hindu in Trinidad recently indicated to me that among some Hindus, even those living in the Western world, the sun has never lost that status.

Another important link comes from the fact that most of the sacrificial victims throughout the centuries—whether in South Pacific island villages, at Tenochtitlan, or in Rome's Coliseum—have been selected from among those who were the enemies of those offering the sacrifice, and by extension, enemies of the god.

Satan's grand scheme of pitting petty, imaginary gods against each other to provoke wars and human sacrifice has been successful for millennia. It still works in such places as Lebanon and Ulster, where people imagine that they are serving Yahweh or Allah by blowing other human beings to smithereens. Is it really too farfetched, then, to imagine that Satan will, at some point in the future, seek to reinstitute literal worship-based sacrifice of Christians who refuse to bow the knee to him?

Jesus, who gave the book of Revelation to John, didn't think it too farfetched: "He [the antichrist beast] was granted power to give breath to the image of the beast, that the image of the beast should both speak and cause as many as would not worship the image of the beast to be killed" (Revelation 13:15, NKJV).

Is it possible (dare we say probable?) that Satan is at this very moment marshaling the forces that will one day soon oversee a plan to begin systematically executing, as human sacrifices, the only people who have not been deceived by his master plan—true Christians who have learned to love God and His truth more than life itself? Could such a plan be brought to fruition in our modern world? If so, how can you avoid being deceived by the most practiced deceiver in the universe? How can you ensure that you will be among the elect who will not be deceived when the fire starts to fall?

Just Imagine

As I've said before, it is dangerous to try making specific applications of prophecies. Yet we can see broad outlines of events. What I have tried to do in the following chapter is to paint a possible scenario. Starting with the broad strokes of history and prophecy as my framework, I then filled in details—imagined happenings—to bring the story to life and illustrate what *could* happen.

I want to state emphatically that I do not anticipate that events will transpire in just the way I have described them. In fact, I was fearful of writing this story simply because a story tends to take up a permanent dwelling place in a person's mind, and my story might even begin to be used unwittingly by some as a map for their expectations.

But I think that the best way to draw together the meaning of all the history, current movements, and prophecies we've looked at is to allow our imagination free reign to play with the possibilities and to bring home the implications of what we've seen.

So just imagine that . . .

CHAPTER

11

Abu Bushra and the Pyramid of the Sun

"OK, what's bothering you? Did I put too much salt in the mashed potatoes again, or what?" Sally Winston challenged lightheartedly. "It was your turn to fix supper anyhow, but I was too hungry to wait, so don't complain," she smiled, hoping to bring Kurt out of his unusually pensive mood.

"I'm sorry, honey, I didn't mean to shut you out." Kurt jabbed his fork in his potatoes as he spoke. "I've just got a lot on my mind, I guess."

"I saw you talking to Mr. Johnson. Did you find out how come they've got their house up for sale?"

"Well, yes, kind of . . . I guess. But I'm not sure I really understand. I guess that's what I've been thinking about."

"We haven't done anything to offend them, have we?"

"Oh, no, it's nothing like that."

"What did he say then?"

"Well, it's kind of complicated, and I'm not sure I can explain it. . . . Hey, don't we have a Bible around here somewhere?"

"It's in the bookcase unless you moved it."

Kurt slid his chair back and went for the Bible. When

he returned he opened it and read a few verses, then looked up at Sally. "It *is* in here—just like he said! I don't believe it. How come I never read that before? I mean, I thought I knew all about 666 and the antichrist and that kind of stuff."

"What are you talking about? *What's* in there?" Sally asked.

"OK, you remember the sermon Pastor Wheeler preached three weeks ago?"

"Not really; I probably slept through it," Sally laughed.

"No, not this one you didn't. Remember? We talked about it afterward. He was telling about the revival of the spiritual gift of prophecy, and he told about this great new prophet who's supposed to be working miracles and healing people and stuff in India or someplace."

"Bangladesh."

"OK, Bangladesh—but anyhow, you remember now, don't you?"

"Yeah, I remember. He said that the guy claims to be a reincarnation of the spirit of Abraham, Moses, Elijah, Jesus, Mohammed, Buddha, and a half dozen other notables. Sounded kind of wacko to me." Sally was having a hard time taking Kurt's concern seriously.

"Laugh if you want, but Pastor Wheeler seemed pretty impressed and said we ought to keep our eyes on this guy. He said that it used to be just the New Agers who paid attention to him, but that now he's getting worldwide attention. He said that even the pope sent a delegation to talk with him and that the leaders of some of the Orthodox and Protestant churches were considering doing the same."

"Yeah, so what does that have to do with the Johnsons moving? They don't really seem like the type to go traipsing off to Dacca to grow their hair long and kiss some guru's toes.''

''Well, Mr. Johnson says that their moving is based on their understanding of Bible prophecy. And this is where it gets complicated,'' Kurt said, shoving his plate aside. ''You remember that the pastor said to watch this guru or prophet or whatever? Well, last week I saw a write-up about him in a magazine at the office, so I read it.

''It said that he's really getting a lot of attention now and that even some Muslim and Buddhist and Hindu scholars are starting to proclaim him a genuine prophet because of the miracles he works. Then it said—and here's the thing that Johnson was talking to me about—that this guy, Abu Bushra, has promised that within six months he will perform one great sign to prove that God has sent him as a messenger to the world for today.

''The article said that there's a lot of speculation about what the sign might be and quoted some Catholic theologian as saying that the acid test of prophets in Old Testament times was the ability to call down fire from heaven.''

''So the Johnsons think he's gonna rain fire down right here in our little neighborhood, and they're getting out while the getting's good, huh?'' Sally interjected.

''No, no, can't you take anything seriously?''

''Hey, I just wish you'd quit being so somber about the whole thing. Prophets come and prophets go—especially those freaky New Age kinkos. I learned a long time ago not to pay any attention to any of them. What did Johnson say to get you so worked up?''

''Well, I saw him in the driveway when I went out to get the mail, so I waved at him and asked when they planned to move and where. He said it was a long story and asked if I had a few minutes for him to explain.''

''And that's how come *I* got to fix dinner!''

"Yes, dear, that's how come you got to fix dinner," Kurt was smiling at last. "Well, Johnson asked me if I'd heard anything about this Abu Bushra guy, and I told him what Pastor Wheeler had said and what I'd read about him. Then he dropped the bombshell. He said that he thought that Abu Bushra could be . . . well . . . not the antichrist actually, but a prophet to lead people to the antichrist. Or he could even be Satan in human form. Johnson said that he was moving his family out to the country so they would be safer in the tribulation, or time of trouble, or something like that."

"Wait a minute! You're saying that our pastor and everybody up to the pope thinks this guy is God's greatest gift since Moses, but that Johnson thinks he's the antichrist? Boy, this guy's really mixed up!"

"OK, yeah, that's what I thought at first too. But then he asked me if I'd heard the part about the sign being the ability to call down fire from heaven. Of course I told him I had, so then he said that in the last days that would actually be the sign of the antichrist, and he told me to go home and read Revelation 13:11-18.

"Here it is, right here in verse 13: 'And he doeth great wonders, so that he maketh fire come down from heaven on the earth in the sight of men,' and then if you read on down to verse 18, you find out that this is the same power that makes people take the mark of the beast and that has the number 666!"

"Well, that's all very interesting," Sally replied. "But has this guy really said he's going to bring down fire from heaven? Or is that just somebody's speculation?"

"That's exactly what I asked Johnson. And do you know what he said?"

"What?"

"He said that that's not the point. He said the point is that all the religious leaders are being caught up by this guy and think that the very thing that is a sign of the antichrist is a sign of God's prophet. So Johnson thinks that the antichrist could appear anytime and even the church leaders would be led astray and begin to persecute anybody who wouldn't bow down to him.

"He said there are lots of other prophecies that point to the same sort of thing and that it's especially frightening to see the leaders of a whole bunch of different religions listening to the same teacher, because that's what the Bible predicts will happen in the time of the antichrist."

"That seems like proof enough to me that the guy's got his head screwed on backward," Sally said. "I mean, they seem like nice people and all that, and they don't make any trouble in the neighborhood. But if you ask me, what this world needs is a little more unity and cooperation and a lot fewer disagreements over such things as religion. And now Johnson says that when the religions start to agree, that's the work of the antichrist? Boy, that's too much for me to swallow. I hope their house sells quick . . . *real* quick! Somebody oughta call down fire on *their* house!" Sally was only half joking now.

The following week the Johnsons invited Kurt and Sally over to study some of the prophecies. Sally wanted nothing to do with it, so she had Kurt make excuses for her.

Kurt was fascinated with what he heard and went back every Tuesday night for several weeks. He tried to share what he was learning with Sally, but she wasn't interested. "Look, when and if this Abu Bushra, or anyone else, succeeds in calling down fire from heaven, then I'll get interested in what the Johnsons have to say," she proclaimed. "Until then, it's just one religious kook's word against the other's, as far as I'm concerned."

A few weeks later Abu Bushra came to the United States

on a teaching and healing mission. Soon he was drawing large crowds of government workers and even a few congressmen to lunch hour lectures near the foot of the Washington Monument in Washington, D.C. On visits to St. Elizabeth's and other hospitals, he restored sanity to the mentally disturbed and even cured several AIDS patients who had not responded to the latest antiviral drugs.

The crowds grew so large that he finally had to go into hiding and speak only via the facilities of the Trinity satellite television network. Its board of directors, made up of representatives from many different Christian denominations, made its facilities available to him as a show of ecumenical support.

Then on May 15 came the announcement that shook things loose at the Winston household. It came via the usual channels, but was picked up and rebroadcast on all the other networks' evening news programs.

"Because there has been a lot of controversy and disagreement among religious leaders as to the nature and source of my power, I will, on June 21, 2012, at the time of the last summer solstice in the Northern Hemisphere before the end of the 5,125-year-long Mayan Great Cycle, perform a miracle that will show to all religions that I am the reincarnation of their greatest leaders. This will be in preparation for the dawn of the New Age at the end of the Great Cycle, which will come at the time of the summer solstice in the Southern Hemisphere.

"To understand what my sign will be, study the ways of the Mayas and Aztecs. And consider how the God of the Christians and Jews manifested His power in the days of Moses and Elijah."

Kurt and Sally saw the broadcast on *NBC Nightly News*. After broadcasting Abu Bushra's statement, the network cut to a live three-way satellite hookup with an anthropologist in Mexico City, a rabbi in Jerusalem, and a Roman

Catholic scholar at Georgetown University. All were taking a rather philosophical approach to the issue. No one was willing to make a statement either supportive or particularly critical of Abu Bushra. But they all agreed that the miracle he had alluded to must involve calling down fire from heaven.

When the network cut to a commercial, Kurt pushed the mute button on the remote control and asked, "Well, what do you make of that?"

"I said it before, and I'll say it again," replied Sally. "When somebody really does call down fire from heaven, then I'll get interested."

"I just wish the Johnsons were still here. I'd like to hear what they have to say about *this*," Kurt said.

The following Sunday Pastor Wheeler preached a sermon based on various Old Testament examples of fire coming down from heaven. In conclusion he said he knew there was a lot of excitement now over Abu Bushra, but that he thought it was a bit premature. "Sure, everything looks right at this point," he said. "But I think the acid test will come on June 21. Let's not jump to any conclusions before we see what happens then. But if he actually does call down fire from heaven, then I think the Scriptures are clear in saying that this is God's messenger—the one who is to prepare the way for the ushering in of His kingdom on earth. In the words of Malachi the prophet: 'Behold, I will send you Elijah the prophet before the coming of the great and dreadful day of the Lord.'

"I say to you today: We will know Elijah when he does the works of Elijah. Let him bring fire from heaven if he is the one!"

The Pyramid

A cool front from Canada blew through Washington, D.C., on June 20, giving the residents a welcome respite

from the 90-degree days and high humidity that charac-
terize much of the summer there.

June 21 dawned with clear, blue, cloudless skies. The
weather forecasters were unanimous in predicting an ideal
day, with temperatures in the upper 70s and no chance
whatever of rain or thunderstorms.

Abu Bushra's followers had gotten special permission
to erect a concrete block platform on the Mall between the
Washington Monument and the Capitol. Crowds mingled
around it for several days prior to the sixteenth. Several
thousand people slept on the Mall the night of the twentieth to assure good positions from which to observe the
next day's activities.

Kurt and Sally considered making the trip to Washington, but in the end elected to watch the event on TV.
Because of the amount of interest generated, all three
major networks plus CNN, the BBC, the CBC, and a host
of other foreign broadcasters planned to give the event live
coverage starting at 8:00 a.m. Eastern Daylight Time.

The Winstons chose NBC as the main channel to
watch, but from time to time Kurt would use the digital
features of the TV to put two or three other networks'
coverage on the screen simultaneously.

"I'm standing at the base of the immense platform that
has been erected by the followers of Abu Bushra on the
Mall in Washington, D.C.," reported news anchor Dan
Coffey as the camera zoomed out from a closeup on his
face to take in his surroundings.

"The platform, as you can see, is about 20 feet high
and built in the shape of a pyramid with its capstone
missing. If you have a dollar bill in your pocket, you might
want to just turn it over and look at the back. On the
left-hand side you will find a picture of the Great Seal of
the United States of America. What we have here seems to
have been constructed as a replica of the pyramid on the

back of the seal, with a couple exceptions. There is no "flying eye" above this pyramid, and the pyramid on the Great Seal has 13 tiers. This one has 14. Also, at the base of the great seal appear the Roman numerals MDC-CLXXVI, which, of course, denote 1776, the year of the founding of the United States. This pyramid has MMXII, which denotes the current year 2012.

"On the flat surface at the top of the pyramid you can see a brightly polished copper kettle or caldron. It is our understanding that the caldron will be filled with distilled water and that Abu Bushra believes he can call down fire from the sky that will literally burn up the water.

"I have here with me a representative of Abu Bushra's organization. He identifies himself simply as Sunsee, and he says he is here to tell us about the significance of the pyramid and its relationship to the Great Seal.

"Mr. Sunsee, this certainly is an interesting structure that your organization has built here. Could you tell us a little bit about this capless pyramid and the significance of the symbolism connected with it?"

Sunsee appeared to be in his early 40s, about five and a half feet tall and perhaps of Oriental or mixed Oriental-Caucasian descent. His close-cropped hair gave the impression that his head might have been shaved two or three weeks ago. He was dressed in a white robe that reminded Kurt of a Roman toga. He spoke good English with just a hint of a British accent. He had walked up beside Dan Coffey when he heard his name mentioned and now stood facing directly into the lens of the camera. His face remained passive as he spoke.

"Yes, Mr. Coffey. Abu Bushra has sent me here to enlighten the American people and the people of the world concerning the significance of the pyramid. It always amazes me to talk with Americans and to ask them about their Great Seal. I have found that very few have any idea of the meaning of the symbols on the seal. But this seal had great significance to the founding fathers of this nation. It is a tragedy that people do not understand this.

"First of all, I will explain the significance of the Great Seal. Then I will explain the significance of the pyramid Abu Bushra has built here." The camera now zoomed out to reveal that an easel with a picture of the Great Seal had been placed beside Sunsee.

"Notice that the pyramid on the seal has no capstone, but that what you called a flying eye is just above it and supplies its capstone. The pyramid anciently, as developed by the Egyptians, represented the rebirth of their world after the annual flood of the Nile. Pyramids to them were originally just an extension of the primordial hillock—the first thing to appear above the waters each year." Sunsee was not pointing at the seal, but continued staring straight at the camera. It seemed to Kurt that he might be reciting something he had rehearsed many times.

"The founding fathers had the pyramid on the seal constructed with 13 tiers. Now, this is not only symbolic of the 13 states; the number 13 is traditionally the number of transformation and rebirth.* The inscription below the pyramid reads *'Novus Ordo Seclorum.'* "

"I believe that translates 'A new order of the world,' " Coffey broke in, apparently eager to demonstrate that he had not lost control of the interview, which was turning into a monologue.

"This Latin phrase translates into English as 'A new order of the world,' " Sunsee continued, as though he had not even heard his interviewer. "This country's founding

---

* The explanation of the meaning of the great seal given here is based on an explanation given by Joseph Campbell on the Public Broadcasting System's series *The Power of Myth*. In the 1980s Campbell ranked as one of the two most popular authors among New Age readers. See Joseph Campbell with Bill Moyers, *The Power of Myth* (New York: Doubleday, 1988), pp. 25-29.

fathers believed that in 1776 they had founded what we today would call a New Age.

"The eye at the top of the pyramid symbolizes what they believed would be the key to the success of this new order they had founded. The eye represents the eye of God, which was to them the eye of reason. The symbolism here is most potent. Consider the pyramid. When one is at the base of the pyramid, he is on one of its four sides. But as people on the various sides ascend toward the top, they grow closer to one another. At the very peak they come together, and there is no more division.

"The founding fathers of this nation believed that the eye of reason was the key to eliminating the divisiveness that has plagued our world with destructive strife. We saw something very similar in the French Revolution, which occurred just a few years after the American Revolution of 1776. The French went so far as to abolish traditional religion and to declare reason their god.

"Further testimony to the founding fathers' fascination with the power of reason is found in the numbers at the base of the pyramid. The number 1776 has a double significance. The obvious allusion is to the year of the signing of the Declaration of Independence. But the founding fathers saw special significance also in the fact that when you add together the four numbers of that year—1 plus 7 plus 7 plus 6—the sum is 21. Twenty-one is traditionally the age of majority, or the age of reason, for human beings.

"So the founding fathers of the United States believed that reason could be their god, and that reason would guide them to unity and peace. As long as America followed this principle, it stayed out of most of the conflicts that afflicted Europe. In his farewell address George Washington pointed this out and pleaded with Congress to avoid getting entangled in the alliances of

Europe. As long as the United States followed this advice, the country was able to exist at the top of the pyramid. But when the U.S. entered World War I, it descended from the top and once again aligned itself with the divisive forces that had caused so much strife through the years.

"The same principles were illustrated in the pyramids built by the Mayas, Aztecs, and others in the Americas. The Aztec great pyramid of Tenochtitlan had temples for two gods at the top, symbolizing the unity of the dualities at the peak of the pyramid. And the Aztecs began each of their new ages—each of their 52-year cycles—with a ceremony on top of a pyramid. In just six months we will hold a celebration in Mexico City to commemorate an event for which the universe has waited more than five millennia! The end of the Great Cycle that began in 3113 B.C. will mark the beginning of the New Age of peace and harmony!

"The strife and bloodshed we see today is the result of people living below the peak of the pyramid and seeing themselves as divided. The world needs to regain the American vision of unity—to realize that we are all really one—to live once again at the top of the pyramid if this New Age is to be peaceful and prosperous—"

"This is very interesting background. I don't think I had ever heard the seal explained that way before," Coffey broke in. "But there are some obvious differences between the pyramid on the seal and the pyramid you have constructed here."

"*Abu Bushra* has constructed," Sunsee corrected the newsman. "Yes, there are differences," he continued. "Very important differences. First of all, you will notice that there are 14 tiers on this pyramid. Furthermore, the number at the bottom signifies our current year 2012. It is also significant that by adding the number 2 to the number 12 you arrive at the number 14.

"The 13-tiered pyramid leading to the god of reason has been known to be a failure for more than two centuries. The French Revolution proved the fallacy of trying to unite under the banner of reason. The various 'reasonable' factions in that revolution could not agree on a reasonable course, so they resorted to the guillotine as a method of severing the reasoning capacities of those who reasoned differently than themselves!

"So today we have a 14-tiered pyramid. There was a level that was needed beyond the 13 tiers leading to reason. This fact has been known, but not widely recognized, for more than two centuries. The fallacy of relying on reason to provide peace and prosperity became common knowledge only in the last half of the twentieth century with the era of disillusionment with the triumphs of technology. Prior to that time people believed that science and human ingenuity and reasonableness could solve the world's problems.

"Out of that era of disillusionment grew the hippie movement of the sixties and the New Age movement that took root in the eighties and has continued to grow in many areas. These movements recalled people to their spiritual roots and made them aware of their need of a guiding power to lead them to peace and prosperity.

"This power is, of course, God. The same God who created this world. The same God who has given us the number 7 to stand for perfection, because on the seventh day of Creation the world and mankind were perfect."

As Sunsee had moved from talking about history and numbers to talking about God, his face had changed from passive to passionate, and his voice had begun to rise in rhythm and pitch. Now as he brought his carefully rehearsed recitation to its climax, he raised his fist and took on the excited mannerisms of a fervent evangelist.

"Today we have constructed a new pyramid. A pyramid with 14 tiers leading us to the top, where unity will be achieved. Founded, not on human reason, but on the number of perfection—the number of God Himself—twice the number of perfection: 14. Fourteen is the number where the dualities of God come together in unity. Fourteen is the number symbolizing the harmony of yin and yang. Fourteen is the number going beyond human reason to reliance on God Himself to bring the world to unity and peace. The pyramid you see here today, which symbolizes the dawn of a new era—the New Age—is founded on this year 2012 and on the number 14."

"Wow!" Dan Coffey was nonplussed and at a loss for words. He looked past the camera for a moment. "I think we're due. . . . Yes, we'll be right back after these important messages."

When Coffey came back after the commercial break, neither Sunsee nor the seal were anywhere to be seen. Coffey was back into his planned script, giving a guided tour around the pyramid and describing the elaborate schemes that various organizations had implemented to ensure that no hoax could be worked to make people think fire had descended from heaven when it had not.

He interviewed a representative from the TRW Corporation who had scraped off a small sample of copper from the caldron and had it flown by helicopter to a metallurgy lab. The representative explained that if the "experiment" was successful, a second sample would be taken and analyzed to see if any chemical changes had occurred.

Coffey then went on to explain that the water for the kettle was being supplied by a nationally known supplier of distilled water for laboratory use. Once the water was in the kettle, it would be sampled and analyzed on the spot by a computer supplied by a manufacturer of swimming pool test equipment.

An organization called Hoax Debunkers' Science Associates had talked Disney Studios into supplying them with eight special high-speed movie cameras that could film the day's events at the rate of 1,000 frames per second so that if anything happened, it could be analyzed in ultra-slow motion. The cameras were set up to film the pyramid from various vantage points—including one atop the Washington Monument—to assure that no sleight of hand could escape observation.

PEPCO, the local electric company, had certified that there were no power lines underground in the vicinity of the platform. And the list of scientific precautions against hoax went on and on.

The networks all sent camera crews into the crowd to interview various types of people about what they expected to happen. One network even tried to interview a dog that its master claimed had psychic powers and would answer questions by lifting its right paw for yes or by lifting its left paw for no. The dog seemed frightened by all the attention, though, and rolled over on its back, lifting both paws. The reporter had a good laugh and said, "Well, if a psychic dog can't predict what will happen here today, who can?"

At precisely 11:00 a.m. Abu Bushra made his grand entry, sitting in a chair that was let down onto the platform from the belly of a helicopter. He gave a long speech detailing why God had called him and given him special powers at this time. It boiled down to the fact that there was too much strife and confusion in the world and that most of it was caused by differences of opinion about religion. "Love is the key to solving these problems," he said. "God is love. And it is to demonstrate God's love that I have performed the healings and other signs. God wants

131

us all to be united and to stop our petty quarrels and disputes."

He went on to inform the listening world that God had decided that it was time to straighten out all the confusion and to bring worldwide unity in preparation for founding His New Age kingdom on earth. He, Abu Bushra, God's personal representative and prophet, was charged with the task of bringing about the unity required. For this reason God had endowed him with special powers, just as God had given special powers to priests and prophets of various religions throughout history.

"It is widely recognized," he said, "that the one special power God has given only to special leaders at special times is the power to bring down fire from heaven. And not just any kind of fire. In the account of Elijah, God's prophet, it is said that the fire could even consume water. That is why we have this kettle of water here today. Today God will demonstrate to all the world that He has called me to lead the world into the New Age of peace and prosperity for all. This will happen at the precise moment when the sun reaches its zenith over Washington, D.C. This will be in exactly 11 minutes and 14 seconds," he said, looking at the technicians manning the high-speed cameras.

"I have with me," he announced, holding up a satchel, "letters from the leaders of several of the world's major religions. Not all have seen fit to be cooperative, but many—including the holy father in the Vatican—have expressed their willingness to cooperate with me in exploring ways to world peace after this demonstration that God has indeed called me as His prophet."

When he had concluded his speech, Abu Bushra stepped back from beside the caldron, assumed a lotus position in one corner of the platform, and appeared to enter a trance as he focused his attention on the kettle.

At the precise moment he had predicted, what appeared to be a tongue of flame descended from the direction of the sun and struck the water. Immediately flames erupted from the caldron. Television cameras zoomed in for a closer look. As the water level in the caldron lowered, the copper above the waterline began to glow bright red. The flames shot higher and higher, and the kettle roared like a jet engine.

It was all over in five minutes. The water was consumed, and as the flames glowed green, the kettle melted into an amorphous blob of glowing metal. Through it all, Abu Bushra had sat unmoving, staring blankly at the unfolding miracle.

The news commentators were speechless. It was as if no one had *really* expected this to happen.

"I go now to the Temple of the Sun that has been erected in the mountains near Boulder, Colorado. I shall speak further from that temple. The news media will be invited to hear my next message on Sunday, June 24."

With that, the helicopter returned and whisked Abu Bushra away.

Kurt and Sally remained glued to the television screen for several more hours as the networks paraded experts and analysts across the screen.

When Kurt finally turned the tube off, he looked at Sally. "Can I tell you now what Mr. Johnson predicted would happen next?" he asked.

"Yeah, I guess so," a subdued Sally replied.

"He predicted that Abu Bushra would require all religions to unite in worshiping God according to his specific instruction—some of which will contradict the Ten Commandments. If that happens, we're getting out of here and going to find the Johnsons."

On Sunday television crews were set up in the Temple of the Sun to record Abu Bushra's next pronouncement. He carefully reviewed the long history of religion on Planet Earth, pointing out how certain aspects of God's character had been revealed in each of these religions. He emphasized that the most consistent point running through almost all religions was the attribution of divine status to the sun. "Most Christians do not realize it," he said, "but even their most basic religious practices derive from sun worship. You can ask the pope or Roman Catholic scholars or any knowledgeable church historian. The Christian day of worship was established as *Sun*day by decree of the Roman emperor Constantine the Great in A.D. 321. It is well known that Christian worship on Sunday originated with Mithraism, an ancient Vedic religion devoted to the sun, which was in honor—to quote the emperor himself—of 'the venerable day of the Sun.' December 25 was also originally celebrated in Mithraism as the birthday of the sun—the day when the ancients offered gifts and sacrifices to the sun to ensure its success in bringing summer back once again."

Based on these facts, Abu Bushra stated that it was God's will that all nations and religions unite in their practice of worship, that he was God's representative who would give instructions for this united worship, and that to begin with, all peoples of the world should listen via television or radio to his instructions from the temple each Sunday.

"Our goal will be to bring about unity in worship of God, and thus unity, peace, and prosperity for the entire world. Each week Sunday will be the day for working toward this goal.

"I will speak to you again one week from today, he concluded. "By the power vested in me by the God of heaven—which power I have manifested by bringing down fire from heaven—I demand that all nations and peoples of the earth hear and obey!"

Kurt sat in stunned silence after the broadcast. Finally he mustered a weak voice. "Where did you put the Johnsons' new address?" he asked.

I've chosen to break off my story right at this point and leave the rest to your imagination, because it is not my intention to make specific predictions, but only to provide a scenario for the fulfillment of prophecy.

In my imagination the rest of the story includes civil enforcement of nationwide, then worldwide universal homage to the power represented by Abu Bushra. It also includes persecution of anyone who won't heed Abu Bushra's commandments, and finally a death decree against all who refuse to accept the new amalgamated religion he proposes. The stage will have been set, by the forces we have studied in this book, for the world to believe that anyone who opposes the movement for world unity should be killed. And there will be no further resistance to the idea of sacrificing (perhaps literally, perhaps simply by executions) these few for the prosperity of the many. The old "me versus thee" syndrome will function just as well in the "New Age" as it has throughout history.

I believe the broad outline of such a scenario is clearly painted in the Bible. But could it really happen?

Could it? I realize that I keep repeating this question. I suppose it is because I can hardly believe it myself. But consider the following chapter before you answer.

CHAPTER
12

Could It
Really Happen?

Could what I have described in the previous chapter really happen? Of course, I don't expect *exactly* what I described to happen. The actual fulfillment of Bible prophecy may not even remotely resemble the specific events I described. Chapter 11 was intended simply to spark people's imagination. The question we must ask ourselves is whether conditions developing in our world are setting the stage for some sort of religious power that opposes God to gain center stage and compel people, under threat of death, to obey its commandments in place of God's as Revelation 13 predicts.

As civilization has developed, our world has become more secular. In recent years people have ridiculed the idea that our planet could ever again be united under one religious ruler. For a time it seemed that the more technologically advanced regions of the world had entered a postreligious era.

The fundamentalist Muslim revolution in supposedly Westernized Iran, the rise of fundamentalist Christianity in the United States, and the concurrent reassertion of spiritualism's power throughout Europe and North America via the New Age movement have demonstrated the fallacy of considering modern society postreligious. In times of uncertainty, or when inspired by a demagogue, people can be easily pointed back to religion as the solution to their problems.

And at the very core of humanity's baser nature lies the propensity to judge that anyone who disagrees with my beliefs should be exterminated. Although the paradigm shift promoted by the New Age movement calls for greater openness and tolerance, I have noted growing signs of lack of tolerance for traditional Western religion. It remains to be seen how long tolerance will be the watchword of those who perceive that their plans are being contested or thwarted by people of an opposing religious persuasion.

The Bible predicts that in the end of time those who have rejected the influence of God's Holy Spirit and looked to themselves for salvation—whether through a New Age inward journey or simply through ignoring God and relying on their own works—will become increasingly self-centered and uncaring.

In the midst of the turmoil brought on by self-seeking, nationalism, wars, plagues, and disasters, Satan will send one last demagogue to attempt to unite the world under his (or could it be *her?*) leadership. Modern rulers from Hitler to Khomeini have proven the value of denoting a given people group as public enemies in order to unite the rest of the citizens behind their demagoguery. Those who have learned to truly love God and His truth, as expressed in His law, will naturally be the focus of the ire of this satanically inspired demagogue.

What Daniel Foresaw

Daniel, the Old Testament prophet who was taken captive from Jerusalem to Babylon in 605 B.C., foresaw how this would come about and what the issues would be. In some of the most startling prophecies in the Bible, he warned us to be prepared to take our stand on the right side of these issues. In Daniel 2 we read of how Daniel was able to tell King Nebuchadnezzar both what the king had dreamed and the significance of the dream. This dream laid the foundation for a number of other visions and dreams that gave Daniel an overview of the history of the world right down to the end of time.

In his dréam Nebuchadnezzar saw an image of a person with a head made of gold, chest made of silver, belly made of brass, legs made of iron, and feet made of a mixture of iron and clay. Then he saw a stone that was cut out without hands roll over the image and smash it to bits. The stone then grew larger and larger until it covered the whole earth.

Daniel told Nebuchadnezzar that this dream signified the Babylonian kingdom and three large empires that would successively replace it and each other. After that, no other human kingdom would unite the world to the same extent. Rather, the kingdoms would be like iron and clay—some strong, some weak. They would be unable to unite, but finally the God of heaven would set up a kingdom, represented by the stone, that would truly take in the entire earth.

Daniel's predictions have come true up to this point. After Babylon came the Medo-Persian Empire, then Alexander's Greek Empire, then the Roman Empire. But since that time, no empire has ruled with the clout of these that went before. So the next thing that should happen, according to this scenario, is the establishment of God's final kingdom.

Other prophecies in the book of Daniel fill in more detail about what will happen before God establishes His kingdom.

Daniel 7 tells of one of Daniel's prophetic dreams. In this dream he saw four beasts that represented the same four kingdoms. But instead of using feet and toes to represent the time after the four kingdoms, the beast had 10 horns on its head to represent the time after the fall of the Roman Empire.

In his dream Daniel became particularly concerned with what happened to these horns. He saw an eleventh horn, a little one, come up among the 10 and pluck up three of the others by the roots. This horn grew larger and began to speak "pompous words" (Daniel 7:8, NKJV). As the dream continued, Daniel saw God exercise judgment against this horn, and finally God's people gained the victory and took over the earth from the powers portrayed by the prophetic beasts and horns. But before that happened, the little horn exercised persecuting power against God's people and tried to "change times and law" (verse 25, NKJV). Interpreters of this prophecy see in it a prediction that the final conflict between the antichrist power and the people of God will revolve around the issue of obedience to God's law. The apostle John, the author of Revelation, recognized this as well. In his letter that we know as 1 John, he addresses the issue of the coming of the antichrist (see 1 John 2:18-23). But before taking up this topic, he made sure that his readers understood how they could know that they were on God's side instead of the antichrist's.

After many years of walking with God and watching the effects of the Holy Spirit's movement on human lives, John realized that the best way for a person to know whether or not he or she was actually walking with God was to examine his or her relationship to God's commandments. "Now by this we know that we know Him, if we keep His commandments. He who says 'I know Him,' and does not keep His commandments, is a liar, and the truth is not in him. But whoever keeps His word, truly the love of God is perfected in him. By this we know that we are in Him" (verses 3-5, NKJV).

For John, the beloved disciple, the apostle who best understood and most clearly proclaimed God's love, the central aspect of the Christian's love relationship with God came down to keeping God's word—His commandments.

At the time of the end, when the antichrist power is fully revealed, Kurt and Sally—and everyone else—will have to decide whether to obey God's law as recorded in the Ten Commandments or to obey human laws that have been set up in opposition to God's laws. The antichrist will work great miracles to convince people that he actually speaks for Christ. (The word *antichrist* means "one who puts himself in the place of Christ.") In the end only those who truly love God and trust His Word more than their own senses and their own instinct for survival will remain loyal to God and His law. Only those who have learned to truly love God's truth will in the end escape deception (see 2 Thessalonians 2:9-12).

This is what the broad strokes of Bible prophecy point to for the future of our world.

Could the scenario of chapter 11 really happen, then? The way is certainly being prepared for something like it. The New Age movement as well as forces within the Christian church are paving the way.

What will you do when it comes down to a question of obeying God's commandments or obeying the authority of human powers? What will you do when the only question that makes any difference anymore is "Am I really willing to lay down my life as a sacrifice rather than disobey God?"

Jesus predicted that times like this would come. Indeed, they have come for multitudes throughout the Christian Era. And the irony is that many—including John

Huss, John Wycliffe, Martin Luther, and Menno Simons—have found themselves under the ban of the Christian church itself for standing up for what they knew God would have them do. And some have even been burned, seemingly as human sacrifices (remember that religious powers have often used their opponents as sacrificial victims), because the religious authorities in power considered them to be enemies of God!

Revelation 13 plainly predicts that just before Jesus comes again there will be a time of trial involving the death penalty for anyone who will not bow to Satan's power and receive the mark of the beast.

Furthermore, those who refuse to receive the mark of the beast will be denied all the normal privileges that allow us to live the life we are accustomed to. In the end there will be a law stating that "no one may buy or sell except one who has the mark or the name of the beast, or the number of his name" (Revelation 13:17, NKJV).

Plainly the issue that will decide between those who are on God's side and those on the side of the antichrist will come down to a question of whom we trust. If our faith in God has developed to the point where we would rather throw ourselves fully into His care than disobey His law, we will be able to remain faithful to Him. If we trust Him to provide for us even in a time when our obedience to God makes us the outcasts of society, unable to transact business or even buy food, we will demonstrate that we have learned Abraham's lesson that "God will provide."

Revelation 14 depicts the character of those who have withstood the temptations of the last days. In addition to following Jesus, the Lamb of God, wherever He goes (verse 4), they "keep the commandments of God and the faith of Jesus" (verse 12, NKJV).

Faith that bears fruit in obedience, as it did in the life of Jesus, is the key to receiving the seal of God instead of the mark of the beast. If a time of trial such as the one pictured in Revelation 13 comes to you, know that God can give you the strength to go through it. Know also that God will not save or condemn you on the basis of what you do. Everyone whom He saves is saved by grace. He only asks that in response you give testimony to His love and power by letting Him empower you to live your life in obedience to Him.

God has promised great and eternal honor to those who have been willing to give their lives for Him. Developments in the world make it appear that the prophecies could be fulfilled soon. Sooner than we think, you or I may be among those who face earth's final test. If so, we can overcome by the grace of the God who calls us to trust Him. The God who, Abraham learned, "will provide!"

C H A P T E R
13

What's a Christian to Do?

As I write these words on December 3, 1989, the world is a very different place than it was when I began this manuscript last August. In fact, it is a very different place than it was a week ago.

During the past four months a noncommunist government has been installed in Poland. During the past month the Berlin Wall that stood for more than a quarter century as a symbol of the divisiveness of world politics has come tumbling down. During the past week Mikhail Gorbachev, the president of the largest and most powerful avowed atheistic government in the world has paid a visit to the pope to ask for his help with the Soviet Union's internal problems. [30]

What does this have to do with the New Age movement, Bible prophecy, human sacrifice, the antichrist, or the end of time? It's hard to say right now. But these events illustrate how rapidly things can change in our world. How quickly events we would never deem possible today can become tomorrow's reality!

Thus far I've confined myself chiefly to observing what is happening in our world and sharing my concerns about where the New Age paradigm shift is taking us. But just being aware is not enough. What can or should a Christian do about all this?

My answer comes under three headings: be aware, be prepared, be a Christian.

Be Aware

Awareness is what *Secrets of the New Age* plus the first 12 chapters of this book have dealt with. As Christians we need to be alert to the world changes that facilitate the fulfillment of prophecy. If we see the world moving closer and closer to a point where a religious power—whether it is a New Age-oriented leader, the Papacy, or a Hindu holy man matters not—is being exalted to a position of power as counselor to the nations of the world, we must be aware that doors that could lead to religious intolerance are being opened.

We should also be aware that the doors opening in Europe and other parts of the world make it easier to spread the gospel, but they also make it easier for New Age philosophy to spread! Awareness will help us seize the opportunities at hand to introduce God to those who have been reared under atheistic governments.

We need to be aware that most of the startling movements toward world peace have occurred since August 16, 1987. An author writing in the fall 1988 issue of a Washington, D.C., New Age tabloid was already giving credit to the Harmonic Convergence for the movements toward world peace that had occurred by that time. Though the Convergence was looked upon with disdain in the world press and even by some within the New Age movement, if the nations manage to cope with the current crises and continue the march toward peace, the old adage "You can't argue with success" will no doubt be invoked by those who would like to see the rest of Jose Arguelles' New Age agenda carried out.

Awareness of what New Age philosophy can do to human values is important for those who want to preserve and promote the Christian view of humanity.

Be Prepared

But we must go beyond mere awareness. Being aware that a Peterbilt truck is bearing down on us at 90 miles per hour is not helpful unless we are prepared to respond. Simply trying to get out of the way of the paradigm shift that is making life more dangerous for us will not work, though. The shift will follow us wherever we go.

We must be prepared to stop it or at least slow its progress. We must be prepared to help people see the reality of good and evil in our world. We must be able to show people how much better God's plan is. We must be able to defend Christianity from those who say that it has only caused strife. There is not space here to deal at length with strategies for accomplishing this. And I'm a bit of a novice at this myself. Most of the training I have received in systematic theology and soul winning has been based on the assumption that the people I would share the gospel with have a basically Christian worldview to begin with.

This must change. We must learn to present Christianity effectively to those who have rejected its basic assumptions. The standard gospel presentation question "If you were to stand before the gates of heaven today, on what basis would you ask God to allow you to come in?" is irrelevant to a person who believes in reincarnation rather than heaven or hell.

I have only recently begun to read the writings of Francis Schaeffer, and I had to lay them aside while preparing this manuscript. But I intend to return to volume 1 of *The God Who Is There* to find more help in making Christianity relevant to those who have rejected or never heard its basic premises. The writings of C. S. Lewis, who became a Christian after being an atheist and who continued to work in a highly secularized environment, can also help here.

But simply knowing what arguments to use will not help if we don't really know our Saviour. Proper preparation for meeting the momentous challenges in the world must start with a daily quiet time of study, prayer, and Bible-centered meditation. Nothing beats the Bible for devotional reading that will help you to truly know your God.

A daily walk with God will also prepare you for the times when, like Abraham, you will have to rely totally on God's promises for your future. The prophecies we have studied make it plain that true Christians will come under condemnation in the end-time and that there will come a time when those who stand up against the antichrist will not be able to conduct business as usual. They won't be able to go to the store and buy daily provisions.

Prepare yourself now by relying on God and learning to see His hand working in your life. Let God lead you away from the materialism and secularism that so easily ensnare us today. Make Him, not things, first in your life now, and when it comes time to abandon the things of the world and rely totally on God's promises, you will have developed the kind of faith that will allow you to continue to walk with God.

The underlying theme behind all our preparations for meeting and enduring the onslaught of New Age philosophy is: Be a Christian about the challenges you face.

Be a Christian

People need to see true Christianity in action. We can

preach all we want. We can broadcast the gospel via satellite to the whole world. But the most effective witness is genuine Christians who care about their neighbors and the rest of the world. If Christianity is to overcome the bad name it gets in the press through wars being fought by "Christian" militia and "Christian" factions, it must be represented by people who live, love, and care as Jesus does.

In an article for *Ministry*, the international journal for clergy that I helped edit, I shared eight strategies for Christians dealing with New Age people. I share them again here in the hope that they will help you as you seek to deal wisely with New Age philosophy and the people who have accepted it.

1. Don't compromise. The easiest way to attract New Age-oriented people to a church would, of course, be to preach New Age philosophy. But the New Age path to spirituality and the Christian path are as different as the paths of Siddhartha and Abram.

Siddhartha, who came to be known as the Buddha— the enlightened one—sought spiritual understanding through the inward journey. Finally, after years of enduring deprivation, he sat down under a tree and vowed not to move until he had achieved enlightenment. Seven weeks later he entered the state of nirvana, in which he came to conclude that there is no God, that life consists chiefly of pointless suffering, and that the best end a human spirit can hope for is to be snuffed out and never again to have to acknowledge its pain.

Abram, who came to be named Abraham—father of a multitude—sought spiritual understanding in exactly the opposite way. Although he was inclined to look within and to rely on his own resources, he learned during his long life to look outside himself for blessing. He learned to look to God to care for him. His great enlightenment is

147

expressed in his assurance to Isaac at the foot of Mount Moriah: "The Lord will provide." Abraham did not look forward to the obliteration of his spirit, but through faith in God he looked forward to living in an eternal city "whose builder and maker is God" (Hebrews 11:10).

New Age religion looks inward, to the god within. Christianity looks outward to the transcendent God who spoke with Abraham and Moses, leading them to turn away from self. Christianity speaks of one Man, Jesus Christ, who lived and died once for the salvation of all who would receive Him. New Ageism speaks of a cosmic Christ or a Christ spirit who has, through the millennia, incarnated in various bodies as a teacher, not as a savior.

Christianity warns of evil spirits and demons who want to take over human bodies and speak lies. New Ageism calls them beneficent spirits who need to use human bodies to channel messages of universal love.

Expectation of a New Age brought in by human cooperation runs contrary to hope for the second coming of Jesus to create a whole new world free from the contamination and sin we witness all around us.

There can be no compromise between two such diametrically opposed systems of belief. No melding can preserve Christianity's unique, powerful message for the world.

2. *Help people find God*. Abraham's spiritual journey was successful because he kept following after God until he came to know Him as a friend. When people come to the church as spiritual seekers, we need to help them follow after God as Abraham did.

Many New Age-oriented seekers have little or no background in Christianity. We must be equipped to help them become, not just a part of the church, but children of God. It is easier to offer rituals, church offices, and a seat in the choir than to take the time to lead a person to truly know God through Bible study, meditation, prayer, and shared testimony.

If we are content merely to help seekers find solace in religious activities, we will not have truly satisfied the longing that sent them on their spiritual quest. They may become a part of the church, but until their spiritual longings are satisfied in a growing, knowing relationship with God, they will continue seeking and may fall into occult spiritual teachings because the church has not met their needs.

3. *Reveal the love of God.* Our efforts here must be two-pronged. Both our preaching and our lives must be brought into closer harmony with the love of God as Jesus reveals it.

Many of the people who are involved in the New Age movement have rejected Christianity because they think it presents a God who delights in eternally torturing anyone who rebels against Him. The inaccurate portrayal of God's character inherent in the doctrine of eternal torment drives people away from God and into the arms of channels who proclaim that there is no judgment and that we are all a part of the eternal God.

The more biblically defensible doctrine of the ultimate destruction of the wicked by the fire that will finally cleanse the universe of sin (cf. Matthew 10:28; 2 Peter 3:7-13; Malachi 4:1-3) provides a more accurate picture of God—One who woos sinners rather than drives them away in search of something more pleasing.

But we need to do more than preach God's love. We need to live it out in our lives. In a recent interview Sir George Trevelyan, a leading New Age proponent from England, shared with me his observation that brotherly love is becoming an important issue in the New Age movement. "In fact," he said, "a lot of hugging goes on at most New Age gatherings these days."

People want to belong to groups that provide loving, accepting fellowship and are involved in changing our world for the better. The church should be foremost in demonstrating this type of love, fellowship, and concern.

4. *Let God speak.* Those who search for spiritual light today often become captivated by a channel who speaks messages for a supposedly munificent discarnate being. The captivating power of channels lies in their ability to give authoritative spiritual guidance from a supernatural source.

Christianity has, in the Bible, an authoritative, supernaturally given source of spiritual guidance. A church that wants to attract people who are seeking guidance needs to let God's Word speak to and through it. This leaves no room for rationalization or pandering to the desires of those who are unwilling to submit to the will of God.

When the church speaks unashamedly, unequivocally for God, people will listen.

5. *Show concern for physical as well as spiritual health.* Many people's first contact with New Age ideas comes as a result of a health problem. Discontented or disillusioned with the medical establishment, they seek alternate therapies. If they find relief through treatment by a holistic health practitioner, they often become open to learn about the practitioner's philosophy of life, which may be distinctly New Age.

Many Christian churches have tended to concern themselves with spiritual matters and have, in practice if not in doctrine, denied that a healthful lifestyle has anything to do with spirituality.

But holism (or wholism) is the watchword of the day in our world, and not only among New Age devotees. People realize now that it is impossible to treat one aspect of a person's life without having an impact on all other aspects. A Christian wholistic approach to health must deal with such issues as diet, use and consumption of tobacco and alcohol, exercise, and temperate use of physical energies if we are to be able to help people optimize their spiritual and physical lives.

6. *Show concern for our planet.* Most people who are part of the New Age movement are concerned with ecology. They fault the church for extending the "Protestant work ethic" to the point that Christians have not spoken out against capitalistic ventures that wound our environment. They think that Christians live for "pie in the sky by and by" and that we aren't concerned about depletion of resources, fouling of water supplies, or poisoning of the ocean because we figure God is going to make all things new anyhow.

But Adam and Eve were placed on this planet to tend and keep it. Good stewardship demands that Christians exercise great care to preserve the resources that God has placed at our disposal. It we take this responsibility seriously and begin to speak out on environmental issues, and if we begin to act with an ecologically attuned conscience, this will help New Age-oriented people to realize that we are not so heavenly minded as to be of no earthly good.

Of course, environmental concerns must not become our chief focus. As I will note in my seventh point, we must continue to proclaim strongly that the only real hope for permanent solutions for our world lies in trust in God and His promise to make all things new.

7. *Show concern for people.* The New Age movement has been accused of narcissism and with looking out only for "number one." This accusation, though, is based largely on observation of only the most public and conspicuous aspects of the movement—the commercial ventures that appeal to people's desire to get ahead in life. Many people

within the movement are genuinely concerned with helping others.

The church, of all institutions, should be known for sharing this concern. And most churches do reach out with help for the helpless. But in these days of disproportionate distribution of the world's resources and increasing disparity between the opportunities available to the rich and poor, this needs to be an especially high-priority item. After all, Jesus' final parable, according to Matthew's Gospel, warned of the perils of being so involved in religiosity that we ignore the needs of the hungry, thirsty, the aliens, naked, sick, and imprisoned (see Matthew 25:31-46).

Making this a high priority item will strengthen our credibility with the spiritual seekers in the world.

8. *Believe in and preach the hope of the Second Coming.* New Age hopes fade into mere shadows beside the glorious, blessed hope provided in Jesus' promise to return and make all things new. Christians have a hope that is not based on wishful thinking about some nebulous transformation of consciousness that will make people treat their neighbors better.

The hope of the Second Coming is based on the promises of the Son of God, who cared enough to leave heaven and come to earth to suffer and die, even though He didn't have to. We can and should steadfastly and with great assurance preach the message that He will return again.

The Second Coming hope, or what I like to call the New Earth hope, takes away the need of a New Age hope or a New Age movement.

Replacing the New Age Movement

If Christian churches will carefully, creatively, and under the guidance of the Holy Spirit address and take action on the concerns I have listed above, the New Age movement should pose no threat to Christianity.

It is the churches' failure to address these issues that makes room for the New Age movement to grow by winning converts. Christianity could just as well be benefiting from the energy of the people who are joining New Age organizations. But we must first let people know that they can find genuine spiritual—and other—help within the church. We must let them know that they will not be judged and condemned when they enter the doors of our churches. We must let them know that we are not just pious moralists who want to take away all their freedoms and fun. We must let them know that we care about them, about the world we live in, and about God.

If we can do that, then we should be able to lead them to know and serve and love the God who has promised a new earth, and not just a New Age. Then the new earth movement can replace the New Age movement.

References

[1] *Encyclopaedia Britannica*, Macropaedia, vol. 2, p. 551.

[2] Jose Arguelles, *The Mayan Factor: The Path Beyond Technology* (Santa Fe, N. M.: Bear and Co., 1987), p. 210.

[3] Steven S. H. McFadden, "One Year After the Harmonic Convergence," *Pathways* (a New Age journal published in Washington, D.C.), Fall, 1988, p. 25.

[4] Arguelles' thesis is explained in *The Mayan Factor*. In a forum conversation held on the Compuserve electronic network September 6, 1987, he wrote the following: "I believe that as we approach 2012 that telepathic communication among all members of the race will be reestablished. Notice I say reestablished since I believe that mental telepathy was originally a unique shared trait of the species. The experience of mental telepathy will be greatly aided by the arrival of extraterrestrials sometime after 1992."

[5] Marilyn Ferguson, *The Aquarian Conspiracy* (Los Angeles: J. P. Tarcher, Inc. [distributed by Houghton Mifflin], 1980), p. 23.

[6] James G. Frazer, *The Golden Bough* (New York: Avenel Books, 1981), vol. 1, pp. 387, 388. Frazer's information came from the book *Memorials of Service in India*, by Major S. C. Macpherson, who was a British officer charged with responsibility for stopping the sacrifices.

[7] Joseph Campbell and Bill Moyers, *The Power of Myth* (New York: Doubleday, 1988), p. 106. This book is in the form of an interview by Bill Moyers of Joseph Campbell, and here Moyers is quoting a passage from another book by Campbell, but the book is not identified. The material in square brackets is inserted in an attempt to help the sense of the sentence, which is confusing without it.

[8] Lawrence E. Stager and Samuel R. Wolff, "Child Sacrifice at Carthage— Religious Rite or Population Control?" *Biblical Archaeology Review*, January/ February 1984, p. 32.

[9] Nigel Davies, *Human Sacrifice in History and Today* (New York: William Morrow & Co., 1981), p. 47.

[10] In Davies, p. 46.

[11] *Ibid.*, p. 44.

[12] *Ibid.*, p. 277.

[13] *Ibid.*, p. 75.

[14] *Ibid.*, pp. 290, 291.

[15] Douglas R. Groothuis, *Unmasking the New Age* (Downers Grove, Ill.: Inter-Varsity Press, 1986), p. 18.

[16] *Ibid.*, p. 19.

[17] Davies, p. 19.

[18] *Ibid.*, p. 281.

[19] Lori Heise reported this phenomenon in an article in *Utne Reader*: "A frequent scam is to set the women [sic] alight with kerosene, and then claim she died in a

kitchen accident—hence the term bride-burning. . . .

"In both urban Maharashtra and greater Bombay, 19 percent of all deaths among women 15 to 44 years old are due to 'accidental burns.' In other Third World countries such as Guatemala, Ecuador, and Chile, the same statistic is less than 1 percent" (Lori Heise, "The Global War Against Women," *Utne Reader*, November/December 1989, p. 42).

[20] Davies, p. 290.

[21] For an explanation of channeling, see the chapter "Channels and the New Age," in *Secrets of the New Age*.

[22] "Absentee God?" *Newsmakers*, vol. 1, No. 2, from the editors of *Christianity Today*.

[23] Quoted in Jean Marie Angelo, "Trusting Your Inner Power: Shakti Gawain," *East West Journal*, November 1989, p. 46.

[24] Gilbert M. Grosvenor, "Will We Mend Our Earth?" *National Geographic*, December 1988, p. 770.

[25] Pat Pulling and Kathy Cawthon, *The Devil's Web* (Lafayette, La.: Huntington House, 1989), pp. 53, 54.

[26] Margot Adler, *Drawing Down the Moon* (Boston: Beacon Press, 1979), p. 178.

[27] *Ibid.*, p. 177.

[28] Spangler relates this story in one of his most recent books, but does not reveal the name of either the channel or the Christian, and I have chosen not to reveal the names either to protect his confidence. See David Spangler, *The New Age* (Issaquah, Wash.: Morningtown Press, 1988), p. 4.

[29] A recent survey revealed that 48 percent of the evangelical theologians in the United States "have abandoned the popular early-twentieth-century view that evolution is a denial of God's Creation" (in James Hunter, *Evangelicalism* [Chicago: University of Chicago Press, 1987], p. 33).

[30] I submit the following as a sidelight. I am not certain of its significance. In *Channeling in the New Age*, David Spangler, the author who wrote *Revelation: The Birth of a New Age*, based on channeled material he received at Findhorn in Scotland (see *Secrets of the New Age*, pp. 23-28), wrote the following: "There is no question that in an altered state, information can be gained that comes from somewhere but which reaches the mind of the channel as if from nowhere. I have had many experiences of this nature. For example, in the early eighties, John [one of the entities who spoke to Spangler in channeling sessions] mentioned to me during a channeling that profound political changes were soon to take place in the Soviet Union that would ultimately lead to a different system of government than they have now. He said that Andropov, who was then premier, would soon die, that he would be replaced by an interim caretaker leader, and then that a man named Gorbachev would take over. Gorbachev, John said, would over time initiate radical changes in the Soviet system that would begin to transform the Russian state."